Fun Hats

DELIGHTFUL AND AMUSING HATS TO KNIT, WEAR AND LOVE

Fun Hats

DELIGHTFUL AND AMUSING HATS TO KNIT, WEAR AND LOVE

LYNNE ROWE

Search Press

This edition published in 2013 by
Search Press Ltd
Wellwood
North Farm Road
Tunbridge Wells
Kent TN2 3DR
www.searchpress.com

A Quintet book
Copyright © 2013 Quintet Publishing
Limited
All rights reserved.
QTT.WHK

ISBN: 978-1-84448-933-6

This book was conceived, designed
and produced by
Quintet Publishing Limited
6 Blundell Street
London N7 9BH

Art Director: Michael Charles
Designer: Bonnie Bryan
Photography: Lydia Evans
Illustrator: Bernard Chau
Managing Editor: Emma Bastow
Project Editor: Margaret Swinson
Publisher: Mark Searle

Printed in China by 1010 Printing
International Limited

10 9 8 7 6 5 4 3 2 1

Contents

Introduction

I cannot remember a time when I didn't knit. Like many knitters, my Nan taught me the basics when I was very small. The speed of her knitting fascinated me and I'd watch in awe as she produced the most beautiful things from a simple ball of yarn and two knitting needles.

I was overjoyed when she bought me a children's knitting kit with red plastic needles and brightly coloured yarns, and with these simple tools and her help, I proudly crafted scarves, skirts and hats for my dolls and teddies. There may have been a few holes here and there, but that didn't faze me and eventually, during my teenage years, I progressed to knitting myself jumpers. Well, actually that's not quite true as I do not ever recall finishing a single project. Despite spending lots of my hard-earned cash on gorgeous yarns from my local yarn shop, the only things I seemed to produce were UFOs ('UnFinished Objects' to those new to knitting). In the early 1980s I bought the iconic *Patricia Roberts Knitting Book*, which was packed full of fabulous patterns and accessories. I intended to knit them all. Sadly, I quickly grew bored with the rows and rows of knitting that were needed to produce just the front of a jumper, let alone the back and sleeves. So I left knitting on the back burner for a number of years, apart from knitting my three children the odd cardigan, jumper or hat. I realised that quick, simple and satisfying projects are just up my street.

Then, about five years ago, I suddenly had the urge to knit again. I rummaged out my knitting needles and yarns and started knitting tea cosies which I sold for charity. I can safely say I was completely hooked and started designing my own patterns for fun and quirky, quick knits for those knitters who, like me, are easily bored or put off by larger projects. Now, I am lucky enough to design full-time and I love it, even though it's a dramatic change from my 20-year career as an environmental scientist.

I've designed the hats in this book to be cute, fun and quirky, and I am sure you'll enjoy knitting them as much as I enjoyed designing them. I'm looking forward to seeing lots of little heads sporting fun hats, which I hope will make you smile too, so I encourage you to take out your needles and release your inner knitter. Have fun and remember that you are in charge, so feel free to add some individual touches here and there to make your own unique creations.

Lynne Rowe

Fun Hats

12

14

16

20

24

28

30

32

36

40

44

46

48

50

52

54
58
60
64

66
68
70
74

76
80
82
86

92
96
100
102

Just plain wacky

If you want to turn heads then this section is the thing for you! These crazy designs are not for the faint-hearted. They are sure to attract attention when you are out and about. Knit a wacky beehive adorned with buzzy bees, or an eye-catching mushroom with big white spots. For a unique topper, how about an eight-legged octopus or a funky mohawk? They will all keep little heads toasty on cold winter days.

Mushroom

Here's a hat for a little one who just keeps growing and growing. Keep them warm under this bright mushroom.

Finished Circumference

32.5 (35, 40, 45, 49)cm or 13 (14, 16, 18, 19½)in
To fit up to 6 mths/6–12 mths/12–18 mths/toddler to child/child to pre-teen

Construction

Knitted in the round

Techniques

Cast on, cast off, knit, purl, increase (KFB), decrease (K2tog), knitting in the round, knitting with DPNS

Materials

Yarn

King Cole Merino Blend DK:
• 1 x 50g (1¾oz) ball Aran (46) – MC
• 1 x 50g (1¾oz) ball Clerical (49) – CC1
• 1 x 50g (1¾oz) ball Scarlet (09) – CC2

Needles

• 3.75mm (US 5) circular needles
• 4mm (US 6) circular needles, 40cm (16in)
• Set of 4 or 5 4mm (US 6) DPNS

Notions

• Large square of white washable felt for spots
• White sewing thread and needle
• Stitch marker

Tension

22 sts and 28 rows to 10cm (4in) using 4mm (US 6) needles or correct size needed to achieve this tension

Instructions

Rib

Using MC and 3.75mm (US 5) circular needles, cast on 72 (78, 88, 98, 108) sts. Join in the round ready to start knitting. Place marker.
Round 1: [K1tbl, P1] to the end. Rep Round 1 until rib measures 6.25 (6.25, 6.25, 7.5, 8.75)cm, 2½ (2½, 2½, 3, 3½)in.

Underside of Mushroom

Cut MC, join in CC1 and change to 4mm (US 6) circular needles.
Next Round: K.
For 32.5 (40, 49)cm, 13 (16, 19½)in sizes:
Next Round: [K1, KFB] to the last 2 sts, [KFB] twice. 109 (133, 163) sts
For 35 (45)cm, 14 (18)in sizes only:
Next Round: [K1, KFB] to the end. 117 (147) sts

For all sizes:
Next Round: [K1, P1] to the last st, K1.
Next Round: [P1, K1] to the last st, P1.
Repeat last 2 rounds for a further 2.5 (2.5, 3.25, 3.75, 3.75)cm, 1 (1, 1¼, 1½, 1½)in. 109 (117, 133, 147, 163) sts

Mushroom Top

Change to CC2, cut CC1. Work 6/8/8/10/10 rounds in st st.
Next Round: [K4 (3, 4, 4, 4) K2tog] to last 1 (2, 1, 3, 1) sts, K1 (2, 1, 3, 1). 91 (94, 111, 123, 136) sts
Next Round: K.
Next Round: [K3 (2, 3, 3, 3) K2tog] to last 1 (2, 1, 3, 1) sts, K1 (2, 1, 3, 1). 73 (71, 89, 99, 109) sts
Next Round: K.

For 35cm (14in) size:
Next Round: K35, M1, K36. (72 sts)
For 13 (16, 18, 19½)in, 32.5 (40, 45, 49)cm sizes:
Next Round: [K35 (15, 31, 107) K2tog] 1 (5, 3, 1) times, K36 (4, 0, 0). 72 (84, 96, 108) sts
For all sizes:
Next Round: K. 72 (72, 84, 96, 108) sts

Decreasing

Transfer stitches evenly between 3 or 4 US 6 (4 mm) DPNS before starting the decrease rounds. Use the spare DPN to start knitting.
Round 1: [K10, K2tog] to the end. 66 (66, 77, 88, 99) sts
Round 2 and every alternate Round: K.
Round 3: [K9, K2tog] to the end. 60 (60, 70, 80, 90) sts
Round 5: [K8, K2tog] to the end. 54 (54, 63, 72, 81) sts
Round 7: [K7, K2tog] to the end. 48 (48, 56, 64, 72) sts
Round 9: [K6, K2tog] to the end. 42 (42, 49, 56, 63) sts
Round 11: [K5, K2tog] to the end. 36 (36, 42, 48, 54) sts
Round 13: [K4, K2tog] to the end. 30 (30, 35, 40, 45) sts
Round 15: [K3, K2tog] to the end. 24 (24, 28, 32, 36) sts
Round 17: [K2, K2tog] to the end. 18 (18, 21, 24, 27) sts
Round 19: [K1, K2tog] to the end. 12 (12, 14, 16, 18) sts

Round 21: [K2tog] to the end. 6 (6, 7, 8, 9) sts
Cut yarn, leaving a long tail.

Thread tail on to a darning needle, thread through remaining sts. Pull tight to close the hole, secure with a few stitches. Weave loose ends into WS; trim.

Spots
Make 5 for 32.5 (35)cm, 13 (14)in sizes, 6 for 40cm (16in) size and 7 for 45 (49)cm, 18 (19½) in size. Cut 10 (10, 12, 14, 14) circles of washable white felt, approximately 2cm (¾in) across (a front and back for each spot). Stitch the front and back of each spot together using whip stitch.

Making Up
Stitch one spot to the centre top hat and stitch the remaining spots evenly over the hat.

Finished Circumference

32.5 (35, 40, 45, 49)cm or 13 (14, 16, 18, 19½)in
To fit up to 6 mths/6–12 mths/12–18
mths/toddler to child/child to pre-teen

Construction

Knitted in the round

Techniques

Cast on, cast off, knit, purl, increase (KFB),
decrease (K2tog), knitting in the round,
knitting with DPNS, making a pleat

Materials

Yarn

King Cole Merino Blend Chunky:
• 2 (2, 3, 3, 4) x 50g (1¾oz) balls Old Gold
 (928) – MC
Scraps of DK yarn for the bees:
• Yellow – CC1
• Black – CC2
• White – CC3

Needles

• 6mm (US 10) circular needles, 40cm (16in)
• set of 5 6mm (US 10) DPNS
• 3.25mm (US 3) needles
• 3mm (US 2.5) needles

Notions

• Locking stitch markers
• Small amount of toy filling

Tension

14 sts and 20 rows to 10cm (4in) on 6mm
(US 10) needles or correct size to achieve
this tension

Beehive

Fly around town in a fun beehive hat covered in bees. This structured hat is knitted in the round to avoid a bulky seam.

Special Instructions

Make pleat (MP): Pick up stitches from the marked Round (e.g. Round 5). Knit them with stitches on the left-hand needle, as follows: * From the marked round, use the tip of your right needle to pick up the horizontal loop from WS of your knitting that is directly in line with next stitch on the left-hand needle. Place picked-up stitch on to the tip of the left needle; knit this stitch together with the next stitch. This joins the two rounds and creates a pleat or fold of knitting. After working approximately 10 stitches, lightly fill the pleat with toy filling. Repeat from * to the end of the round.

Note: If this is too fussy, knit all stitches on the 'Make Pleat' (MP) rounds and hand-stitch each pleat when you have finished knitting the hat. Fold each pleat so Rounds 5 and 15 meet, then stitch together with matching yarn. Repeat for subsequent MP rounds. Fill the pleat with toy filling as you stitch.

Instructions

Using MC and 6mm (US 10) circular needles (or DPNS for smaller sizes), cast on 44 (48, 56, 64, 68) sts. Work in rounds and use a stitch marker to mark the start of each round.
Rounds 1–4: [K2, P2] to the end.
Round 5: Pleat round. Place locking stitch markers at the beginning and end of this round. K.
Rounds 6–14: P.
Round 15: MP.
Round 16: K.
Round 17: K.

Round 18–26: P.
Round 27: MP.
Round 28: K.
Round 29: [K9 (10, 12, 14, 15) K2tog] 4 times. 40 (44, 52, 60, 64) sts
Rounds 30–40: Repeat Rounds 6–16. **For 32.5cm, 13in size only:** go to Round 53. **For all other sizes:** continue.
Rounds 41–52: Repeat.
Round 53: [K3 (3, 4, 5, 6) K2tog] 8 times, K0 (4, 4, 4, 0). 32 (36, 44, 52, 56) sts
Change to 6mm (US 10) DPNS.
Rounds 54–64: Repeat Rounds 6–16. **For 32.5 (35)cm, 13 (14)in sizes only:** go to Round 77. **For all other sizes:** continue.
Rounds 65–76: Repeat Rounds 17–28.
Round 77: [K2 (2, 3, 4, 5) K2tog] 8 times, K0 (4, 4, 4, 0). 24 (28, 36, 44, 48) sts
Round 78–88: Repeat Rounds 6–16. **For 13 (14, 16)in, 32.5 (35, 40)cm sizes only:** go to Round 101. **For all other sizes:** continue.
Rounds 89–100: Repeat Rounds 17–28.
Round 101: [K1, K2tog] 8 (8, 12, 14, 16) times, K0 (4, 0, 2, 0). 16 (20, 24, 30, 32) sts
Rounds 102–112: Repeat Rounds 6–16.
For 32.5 (35, 40)cm, 13 (14, 16)in sizes only: go to Round 125. **For all other sizes:** continue.
Rounds 113–124: Repeat Rounds 17–28.
Round 125: [K2tog] to the end. 8 (10, 12, 15, 16) sts
Cut yarn leaving a long tail, thread on to a tapestry needle. Thread needle through remaining 8 (10, 12, 15, 16) sts, pull tightly to gather the hole closed. Tie off; trim yarn ends.

Bees (make as many as you like)
Using CC1 and 3mm (US 2.5) needles, cast on 6 sts.
Row 1: [KFB] to the end. (12 sts)

Row 2: P.
Row 3: [K1, KFB] to the end. (18 sts)
Row 4: P. Change to CC2, do not cut CC1.
Row 5: K.
Row 6: P. Change to CC1, do not cut CC2.
Rows 7–8: Repeat Rows 5 & 6 in CC1.
Rows 9–10: Repeat Rows 5 & 6 in CC2.
Rows 11–12: Repeat Rows 5 & 6 in CC1.
Rows 13–14: Repeat Rows 5 & 6 in CC2. Cut CC2, continue in CC1.
Row 15: [K1, K2tog] to the end. (12 sts)
Row 16: P.
Row 17: [K1, K2tog] to the end.
Cut yarn leaving a long tail, thread on to a tapestry needle. Thread the needle through remaining 8 sts, pull tightly to gather hole closed. Stitch the seam, matching up stripes. Fill with toy filling, thread yarn through the cast-on stitches to gather the hole closed. Using CC2, stitch two eyes and a smiley mouth to the head.

Wings
Using CC3 and 3mm (US 2.5) needles, cast on 3 sts.
Row 1: KFB, K to last st, KFB. (5 sts)
Row 2: K.
Row 3: Repeat Row 1. (7 sts)
Rows 4–6: K.
Row 7: K2tog, K to last 2 sts, K2tog. (5 sts)
Row 8: K.
Row 9: Repeat Row 7. (3 sts)
Cut yarn, leaving a long tail; thread onto a tapestry needle. Thread needle through remaining 3 sts, pull tightly to gather. Stitch the cast-on edge of each wing to each side of the head on the first black stripe in line with the eyes. Stitch each bee to the hat.

Mohawk

Make heads turn with this funky hat. It is guaranteed to catch eyes and start conversations!

Finished Circumference
32.5 (35, 40, 45, 49)cm or 13 (14, 16, 18, 19½)in
To fit up to 6 mths/6–12 mths/12–18 mths/toddler to child/child to pre-teen

Construction
Knitted in the round

Techniques
Cast on, cast off, knit, purl, increase (M1L, M1R), decrease (K2tog), knitting in the round, knitting with DPNS, attaching fringe

Materials
Yarn
Sirdar Bonus Toytime DK:
- 1 x 100g (3½oz) ball Bright Green (886) – MC
- 1 x 100g (3½oz) ball Bright Orange (981) – CC1

Needles
- 4mm (US 6) straight needles
- 4mm (US 6) circular needles, 40cm (16in)
- Set of 4 or 5 4mm (US 6) DPNS
- 3.75mm (US F, 5) crochet hook

Notion
- Stitch marker
- Pins

Tension
22 sts and 30 rows to 10cm (4in) using 4mm (US 6) needles or correct size needed to achieve this tension

Instructions

Earflap (make 2)

Using MC and 4mm (US 6) needles, cast on 5 sts.

Row 1 (RS): K.

Row 2 (WS): P.

Row 3: K1, M1L, K to last st, M1R, K1. (7 sts)

Rows 4–6: Starting with a P row, st st 3 rows.

Rep Rows 3–6 5 (6, 7, 8, 8) times. 17 (19, 21, 23, 23) sts

Next Row: K1, M1L, K to last st, M1R, K1. 19 (21, 23, 25, 25) sts

Next Row: P1, M1L, P to last st, M1R, P1. 21 (23, 25, 27, 27) sts

Rep last 2 rows until 29 (31, 33, 39, 39) sts are on the needle.

Cut yarn and slide earflap to the bottom of the needle.

Make second earflap as instructed. Cut yarn and leave sts on needle.

Main Hat

Note: When you K across the earflap sts, you will need to swap the left needle to your right hand, knit the earflap stitches, then swap the needle back to your left hand to continue casting on.

Using MC, 4mm (US 6) circular needles and the cable cast on method, cast on 3 (3, 4, 3, 6) sts, K across 29 (31, 33, 39, 39) sts from one earflap, cast on 8 (10, 14, 14, 18) sts, K across 29 (31, 33, 39, 39) sts from remaining earflap, cast on 3 (3, 4, 3, 6) sts. 72 (78, 88, 98, 108) sts. Join in the round ready to start knitting. Place marker.

The hat is worked in st st in the following colour sequence:

4 rounds MC.

4 rounds CC1.

Do not cut yarns after every round. Instead, twist unused yarn around working yarn after every two rounds to carry unused colours up along the inside of the hat. Following the colour sequence above, work 16 (23, 32, 39, 39) rounds in st st.

For 35 (45, 49)cm, 14 (18, 19½)in sizes only:

Next Round: [K11 (47, 25) K2tog] to the end. 72 (96, 104) sts

Decreasing

Transfer stitches evenly between 3 or 4 DPNS before starting the decrease rounds. Use the spare DPN to start knitting. Continue with the 8–round pattern sequence and decrease as follows:

Round 1: K.

Round 2: [K6, K2tog] to the end. 63 (63, 77, 84, 91) sts

Round 3 and every alternate round: K.

Round 4: [K5, K2tog] to the end. 54 (54, 66, 72, 78) sts

Round 6: [K4, K2tog] to the end. 45 (45, 55, 60, 65) sts

Round 8: [K3, K2tog] to the end. 36 (36, 44, 48, 52) sts

Round 10: [K2, K2tog] to the end. 27 (27, 33, 36, 39) sts

Round 12: [K1, K2tog] to the end. 18 (18, 22, 24, 26) sts

Note: Work Rounds 13 and 14 in the same colour as Rounds 9–12.

Round 14: [K2tog] to the end. 9 (9, 11, 12, 13) sts

Cut yarn leaving a long tail end. Thread tail end on to a tapestry needle and gather the remaining sts. Pull tight to close the hole and secure with a few stitches. Weave all loose yarn ends into WS of work and trim.

Mohawk

Lay the hat flat with RS facing. Locate the centre 4 stitches and mark with a pin at either side. Using the crochet hook method, attach 1 strand of MC to each of the centre 4 sts on the first row of the hat (4 strands attached intotal). Each strand should be approximately 12cm (5in) long (to be trimmed later). Next, attach 1 strand of MC to each of the centre 4 stitches on the row above. Repeat this process, attaching corresponding strands of MC and CC1 to the centre 4 stitches of each row, maintaining the stripe pattern. Work upward to the centre top of the hat then continue down the centre back of the hat. Once all strands have been attached, trim the Mohawk neatly to the desired length.

Fastening

If desired, add snaps or popper fastenings to the earflaps to make a chin strap.

Zebra

You are in for a wild ride with this hat! With its crazy stripes and bushy mane, the zebra hat is just the thing for those who like their playtime adventurous and their hair untamed.

Finished Circumference
32.5 (35, 40, 45, 49)cm or 13 (14, 16, 18, 19½)in
To fit up to 6 mths/6–12 mths/12–18 mths/toddler to child/child to pre-teen

Construction
Knitted in the round

Techniques
Cast on, cast off, knit, purl, increase (M1L, M1R), decrease (K2tog), knitting in the round, knitting with DPNS, making a braid, picking up and knitting stitches

Materials
Yarn
Debbie Bliss Cashmerino Aran:
• 1 x 50g (1¾oz) ball Black (300) – MC
• 1 x 50g (1¾oz) ball White (025) – CC1
• Scraps of mohair yarn in black and white for the mane

Needles
• 5mm (US 8) circular needles, 40cm (16in)
• 5mm (US 8) DPNS
• 5mm (US 8) straight needles (for earflaps)
• 4mm (US 6) needles (for smaller ears)
• 3.5mm (US 4) needles (for inner ear)

Notions
• Stitch holder
• Black and white washable felt for eyes and nostrils
• Stitch holder
• Small amount of toy filling
• Black and white sewing thread, needle

Tension
18 sts and 24 rows to 10cm (4in) using 4mm (US 6) needles or correct size needed to achieve this tension

Instructions

Earflaps (Make 2)

Using 5mm (US 8) needles and MC, cast on 3 sts.

Row 1 (RS): K.

Row 2 and all even rows: P.

Row 3: K1, M1L, K1, M1R, K1. (5 sts)

Row 5: Change to CC1. K1, M1L, K to last st, M1R, K1. (7 sts)

Row 7: Repeat Row 5. (9 sts)

Row 9: Change to MC. Repeat Row 5. (11 sts)

Row 11: Repeat Row 5. (13 sts)

Row 13: Change to CC1. Repeat Row 5. (15 sts)

Row 14: P.

Starting with a K row, st st 2 rows. Cut yarn, leaving a 10cm (4in) tail for weaving into work later. Slip sts on to stitch holder then work second earflap. Cut yarn and leave second earflap on needle.

Main Hat

Using 5mm (US 8) circular needles and MC, cast on 6 (7, 9, 11, 13) sts, with RS of ear flap facing, knit across 15 sts of one earflap, turn, cast on 13 (19, 23, 27, 31) sts, turn, with RS of second ear flap facing, knit across 15 sts of remaining earflap, turn, cast on 6 (7, 9, 11, 13) sts. 55 (63, 71, 79, 87) sts. Join in the round ready to start knitting. Place marker. Continue in the round in st st, in repeating pattern of 4 rows alternately in MC and CC1 until hat measures 8.75 (11.25, 13.75, 16.25, 16.25)cm, 3½ (4½, 5½, 6½, 6½)in from cast-on edge of main hat.

Decreasing

Change to DPNS and continue in st st and the 8-row pattern repeat.

Round 1: [K2tog] to the last st, K1. 28 (32, 36, 40, 44) sts

Rounds 2–3: K.

Round 4: [K2tog] to the end. 14 (16, 18, 20, 22) sts

Rounds 5–6: K.

Round 7: [K2tog] to the end. 7 (8, 9, 10, 11) sts

Cut yarn leaving a long tail end. Thread tail end on to a tapestry needle and gather the remaining sts. Pull tight to close the hole and secure with a few stitches. Weave all loose yarn ends into WS of work and trim.

Ears (make 2)

Using 4mm (US 6) needles for 32.5 (35)cm, 13 (14)in sizes, 5mm (US 8) needles for 40 (45, 49)cm, 16 (18, 19½)in sizes.

Using chosen needles and MC, cast on 8 sts, leaving a long tail.

Row 1 (WS): P.

Row 2 (RS): K2tog, K to last 2 sts, K2tog. (6 sts)

Repeat Rows 1–2 once more, so ending with a RS row. (4 sts)

Starting with a P row, work in st st for 9 rows, ending with a WS row.

Next row (RS): [K2tog] twice. (2 sts)

Cast off purlwise, leaving a long tail.

Repeat instructions above, using CC1 and 3.5mm (US 4) needles to make a smaller inner ear. Stitch the outer ear to the inner ear. Fold the lower edges of the ear together and stitch to secure fold. Stitch each ear to the top of the hat, leaving a 1½in (4.5cm) gap between the ears.

Muzzle

Using 4mm (US 6) needles for 32.5 (35)cm, 13 (14)in sizes and 5mm (US 8) needles for 40 (45, 49)cm, 16 (18, 19½)in sizes.

Using chosen needles and MC, cast on 12 sts.

Rows 1–8: Starting with a K row, st st 8 rows.

Row 9: K all sts then pick up and K7 sts along the left side rows ends.

Row 10: P all sts then pick up and P7 sts along right-hand side row end. (26 sts)

Starting with a K row, st st 12 rows. Cast off, leaving a long tail of yarn for stitching the muzzle to the face. Pin the muzzle to the centre-front face, just above the cast-on edge (the cast-off edge of the muzzle is the top edge of the muzzle). Stitch in place using tail end of yarn, stuffing lightly with toy filling as you sew.

Nostrils

Cut out 4 x 1.5cm (½in) long ovals of white felt (2 per nostril). Whip stitch 2 ovals together with matching thread then slip stitch each nostril to each side of the muzzle.

Mane

Cut lengths of black and white mohair for mane and stitch firmly to top of hat between ears.

Eyes

Cut 4 circles of white felt, approximately 2cm (¾in) across (a front and back for each eye). For pupils, cut 2 smaller circles of washable black felt approximately 1cm (½in) across. Stitch each black pupil to the centre of one white eye, using whip stitch and black thread. Stitch the front of the eye to the back using whip stitch and white thread. Stitch each eye to the centre of face 2.5cm (1in) apart.

Braids

Cut 3 x 100cm (40in) lengths of CC1 and 6 x 100cm (40in) lengths of MC.

Using a crochet hook, pull 3 lengths of MC halfway through a stitch at the base of earflap 1. Pull 3 lengths of CC1 halfway through the next st along then pull the remaining 3 lengths of MC halfway through the next st along. You now have 6 pieces of yarn in each of the 3 sections. Secure the hat between your knees and braid or plait the 3 sections of yarn together. Make a knot at the end to secure the braids and trim ends straight.

Finished Circumference

40 (45, 49)cm or 16 (18, 19½)in
To fit 12–18 mths/toddler to child/child
to pre-teen
Note: The above measurements refer to
head sizes and not hat sizes

Construction

Knitted in the round

Techniques

Cast on, cast off, knit, purl, decrease
(K2tog, P2tog, SSK), knitting in the round,
picking up and knitting sts

Materials

Yarn
Artesano Superwash DK:
• 3 (3, 4) x 50g (1¾oz) balls Grey (SFN41) – MC

Needles
• 3.25mm (US 3) circular needles, 40cm (16in)
• 4mm (US 6) circular needles, 40cm (16in)
• Set of 4 or 5 4mm (US 6) DPNS
• 4mm (US 6) straight needles

Notions
• Stitch holder
• Black and white washable felt for eyes
• Black and white sewing thread and needle
• Stitch marker

Tension

22 sts and 30 rows to 10cm (4in) using 4mm
(US 6) needles or correct size needed to
achieve this tension

Octopus

Set a new trend with this eight-legged friend. You could make this wacky hat in pink for a squid hat.

Instructions

Rib

Using MC and 3.25mm (US 3) needles, cast on 86 (96, 106) sts. Join in the round ready to start knitting. Place marker.
Round 1: [K1, P1] to the end.
Repeat Round 1 for 6.25 (7.5, 8.75)cm, 2½ (3, 3½)in.

Main Hat

Change to US 6 (4mm) circular needles. Now work in rows.
Next Row (RS): K32 (36, 40) turn.
Next Row: P64 (72, 80). Continue on these 64 (72, 80) sts only and slip remaining 22 (24, 26) sts on to a stitch holder.
Continue in st st until work measures 17.5 (18.75, 20)cm, 7 (7½, 8)in from start of st st.

Crown

Row 1: K43 (47, 53) Sl1, K1, PSSO, turn.
Row 2: Sl1, P22 (24, 26) P2tog, turn.
Row 3: Sl1, K22 (24, 26) Sl1, K1, PSSO, turn.
Rows 4–27: Rep Rows 2–3 a further 12 times.
Row 28: Rep Row 2.
Row 29: Sl1, K22 (24, 26) Sl1 K2tog, PSSO, turn.
Row 30: Sl1, P22 (24, 26) P3tog, turn.
Repeat Rows 29–30 until all side stitches have been worked and 24 (26, 28) sts remain on needle. Cut yarn, leaving a 10cm (4in) tail end for weaving into work later.

Ribbed Brim

With RS of hat facing, and 3.25mm (US 3) circular needles, rejoin MC to the lower edge stitches and work [K1, P1] rib across these 22 (24, 26) sts, pick up and K34 (40, 46) sts evenly up the side of the main hat, K across the 24 (26, 28) stitches on the top stitch holder, pick up and K34 (40, 46) sts evenly down the next side of the main hat. 114 (130, 146) sts
Continue to work in the round and work [K1, P1] rib for 6 (7, 8) more rounds. Cast off in [K1, P1] rib. Cut yarn and pull through last st. Weave all yarn ends into work and trim.

Tentacles (make 8)

Using MC and 4mm (US 6) needles, cast on 13, 15, 15 sts.
Row 1 (RS): K.
Row 2 (WS): P7 (8, 8) K6 (7, 7).
Repeat the last 2 rows for 13.5cm (6in). 11 (13, 12) sts
Next Row: K2 (3, 3), K2tog, K4 (5, 5), K2tog, K3 (3, 3). 11 (13, 13) sts
Next Row: P6 (7, 7) K5 (6, 6).
Next Row: K.
Next Row: P6 (7, 7) K5 (6, 6).
Repeat the last 2 rows until tentacle measures 8 in (18 cm) from cast-on edge.
Next Row: K1 (2, 2), K2tog, K3 (4, 4), K2tog, K3 (3, 3). 9 (11, 11) sts
Next Row: P5 (6, 6) K4 (5, 5).
Next Row: K.
Next Row: P5 (6, 6) K4 (5, 5).
Repeat the last 2 rows until tentacle measures 25cm (10in) from cast-on edge.
Next Row: K1 (2, 2), K2tog, K2 (3,3) K2tog, K2 (2, 2). 7 (9,9) sts
Next Row: P4 (5, 5) K3 (4, 4).
Next Row: K.
Next Row: P4 (5, 5) K3 (4, 4).
Repeat the last 2 rows 4 times more. 4 (5, 5) sts
Next Row: [K2tog] to the last st, K1.
Cut yarn leaving a long end. Thread end on to a tapestry needle; gather remaining sts. Pull tight to close the hole; secure with stitches. Use tail end to stitch side seam and top of tentacle together using mattress stitch (WS together). Make 7 more tentacles. Pin each to the hat approx 3 rows above neck rib, spacing the tentacles evenly around main hat. Stitch in place using mattress stitch and MC. Cut 4 circles of white felt, approx 2cm (¾in) across (a front and back for each eye). For pupils, cut 2 ovals of black felt approx 2cm (¾in) long. Snip ends of ovals to a point. Stitch each pupil to the centre of one eye, using whip stitch and black thread. Stitch front of eyes to back using whip stitch and white thread. Stitch eyes to centre-front face, in line with crown seams.

Rhymes and tales

Bring out your child's inner mouse or give a budding Peter Pan his very own stylish hat, complete with an eye-catching red feather. Combine a hat and a scarf with the easy-to-make Red Riding Hood and Big Bad Wolf hats that will keep your child warm for a walk in the woods.

Peter Pan

This cute little hat, complete with a red feather, would make the perfect accessory to a costume for Peter Pan.

Finished Circumference

32.5 (35, 40, 45, 49)cm or 13 (14, 16, 18, 19½)in
To fit up to 6 mths (6–12 mths, 12–18 mths, toddler to child, child to pre-teen)

Construction

Knitted flat and seamed

Techniques

Cast on, cast off, knit, purl, increase (M1), decrease (K2tog, SSK), 3-needle cast off, knitting an i-cord

Materials

Yarn

Sirdar Bonus DK:
• 1 x 100g (3½oz) ball Emerald (0916) – MC
Sirdar Toytime Bonus DK:
• 1 x 25g (¾oz) ball Signal Red 977 (or scraps of red DK yarn) – CC

Needles

• 4mm (US 6) straight needles
• 3.75mm (US 5) straight needles
• 2 x 3.75mm (US 5) DPNS for 3-needle cast-off
• 3.25mm (US 3) DPNS (for feather)

Tension

22 sts and 30 rows to 10cm (4in) using 4mm (US 6) needles or correct size needed to achieve this tension

Instructions

Brim

Side 1

Using 3.75mm (US 5) straight needles and MC. Cast on 17 (18, 21, 22, 23) sts.
K 2 (6, 6, 6, 6) rows in garter stitch.
*Next Row: K to last 3 sts, K2tog, K1. (1st dec)
K7 rows in garter stitch.
Repeat from * until 8 (9, 10, 10, 10) sts remain.
Continue in garter stitch until piece measures 16.25 (17.5, 20, 22.5, 24.5)cm, 6½ (7, 8, 9, 9¾)in from cast-on edge. Cut yarn and slip sts on to a 3.75mm (US 5) DPN.

Side 2

Using 3.75mm (US 5) straight needles and MC. Cast on 17 (18, 21, 22, 23) sts.
K2 (6, 6, 6, 6) rows in garter stitch.
* Next Row: K1, K2tog, K to end. (1st dec)
K7 rows in garter stitch.
Repeat from * until 8 (9, 10, 10, 10) sts remain.
Continue in garter stitch until piece measures 16.25 (17.5, 20, 22.5, 24.5)cm, 6½ (7, 8, 9, 9¾)in from cast-on edge.
Place the two brim pieces with WS together. Line up the sts on the two needles and work a 3-needle cast off. Cut yarn and pull through last st. Weave yarn end into work and trim.
With WS together, join the back seam with matching yarn using small running stitches.

Main Hat

Using MC and US 6 (4mm) needles, cast on 72 (78, 88, 98, 108) sts.
Work in st st until hat measures 3.75 (5, 6.25, 7.5, 7.5)cm, 1½ (2, 2½, 3, 3)in.

Decreasing

Row 1: K8 (11, 12, 13, 14) [K5 (5, 6, 7, 8) K2tog] 4 times, [K5 (5, 6, 7, 8) SSK] 4 times, K8 (11, 12, 13, 14). 64 (70, 80, 90, 100) sts

Rows 2–4: Starting with a P row, st st 3 rows.

Row 5: K8 (11, 12, 13, 14) [K4 (4, 5, 6, 7) K2tog] 4 times, [K4 (4, 5, 6, 7) SSK] 4 times, K8 (11, 12, 13, 14). 56 (62, 72, 82, 92) sts

Row 6–8: Repeat Rows 2–4.

Row 9: K8 (11, 12, 13, 14) [K3 (3, 4, 5, 6) K2tog] 4 times, [K3 (3, 4, 5, 6) SSK] 4 times, K8 (11, 12, 13, 14). 48 (54, 64, 74, 84) sts

Rows 10–12: Repeat Rows 2–4.

Row 13: K8 (11, 12, 13, 14) [K2 (2, 3, 4, 5) K2tog] 4 times, [K2 (2, 3, 4, 5) SSK] 4 times, K8 (11, 12, 13, 14). 40 (46, 56, 66, 76) sts

Rows 14–16: Repeat Rows 2–4.

Row 17: K8 (11, 12, 13, 14) [K1 (1, 2, 3, 4) [K2tog] 4 times, K8 (11, 12, 13, 14) [K1 (1, 2, 3, 4) K2tog] 4 times, [K1 (1, 2, 3, 4) SSK] 4 times, K8 (11, 12, 13, 14). 32 (38, 48, 58, 68) sts 4 times, K8 (11, 12, 13, 14). 32 (38, 48, 58, 68) sts

Rows 18–20: Repeat Rows 2–4.

Row 21: K8 (11, 12, 13, 14) [K0 (0, 1, 2, 3) K2tog] 4 times, [K0 (0, 1, 2, 3) SSK] 4 times, K8 (11, 12, 13, 14). 24 (30, 40, 50, 60) sts

3 (4, 5) times. 6 (9, 9) sts

For 40cm, 16in size: cut yarn leaving a long tail. Thread tail on to darning needle, gather remaining 6 sts. Pull tight to close the hole; secure with a few stitches.

For all other sizes: continue.

Rows 38–40: Repeat Rows 2–4.

Row 41: [K2tog twice, K1, [SSK] twice. (5, 5) sts

For 45 and 49 cm (18/19½ in) sizes: cut yarn leaving a long tail. Thread tail onto darning needle, gather remaining 5 sts. Pull tight to close the hole; secure with a few stitches. **For all sizes:** use remaining yarn to stitch side seam. Place the main hat inside the brim, lining up back seams and centre-front. Pin the straight edge of the hat brim to main hat cast-on edge. Whip stitch together.

Feather Quill

Using 3.25mm (US 3) DPNS, and CC1, cast on 4 sts. Work an i-cord for approximately 2.5cm (1in) then cast on 2 sts. (6 sts)

Feather Barbs

Now work in rows on 2 DPNS.

Row 1: [K1, YO, K1, YO, K1] twice. (10 sts)

Row 2 and every alternate row: P.

Row 3: [K2, YO, K1, YO, K2] twice. (14 sts)

Row 5: [K3, YO, K1, YO, K3] twice. (18 sts)

Row 7: [K4, YO, K1, YO, K4] twice. (22 sts)

Row 9: [K5, YO, K1, YO, K5] twice. (26 sts)

Row 11: [K2tog, K4, YO, K1, YO, K4, SSK] twice. (26 sts)

Row 12: P.

Repeat last 2 rows 7 more times.

Row 27: [K2tog, K2tog, K2, YO, K1, YO, K2, SSK, SSK] twice. (22 sts)

Row 28 and every alternate row: P.

Row 29: [K2tog, K2tog, K1, YO, K1, YO, K1, SSK, SSK] twice. (18 sts)

Row 31: [K2tog, K2tog, YO, K1, YO, SSK, SSK] twice. (14 sts)

Row 33: [K2tog, K3, SSK] twice. (10 sts)

Row 35: [K2tog, K1, SSK] twice. (6 sts)

Row 37: [K3tog] twice. (2 sts)

Cut yarn leaving a long tail. Thread tail on to a darning needle and gather the remaining 2 sts. Pull tight and secure with stitches. Use tail end to stitch the side of the feather to the brim (stitching through the brim and main hat). Tie off; trim loose ends.

Rows 22–24: Repeat Rows 2–4.

Row 25: K4 (7, 8, 13, 14) [K0 (0, 1, 1, 2) K2tog] 4 times, [K0 (0, 1, 1, 2) SSK] 4 times, K4 (7, 8, 13, 14). 16 (22, 32, 42, 52 sts)

Rows 26–28: Repeat Rows 2–4.

For 49cm (19½in) size only:

K14, [K1, K2tog] 4 times, [K1, SSK] 4 times, K14. (44 sts)

Repeat Rows 2–4.

For all other sizes: continue.

Row 29: K0 (3, 8, 13, 14) [K2tog] 4 times, [SSK] 4 times, K0 (3, 8, 13, 14). 8 (14, 24, 34, 36) sts

For 32.5cm (13in) size: cut yarn, leaving a long tail. Thread tail onto darning needle, gather remaining 8 sts. Pull tight to close the hole and secure with a few stitches.

For all other sizes: continue.

Rows 30–32: Repeat Rows 2–4.

Row 33: [K2tog] 3 (6, 8, 9) times, [SSK] 4 (6, 9, 9) times. 7 (12, 17, 18) sts

For 35cm, 14in size: cut yarn leaving a long tail. Thread tail on to darning needle, gather remaining 7 sts. Pull tight to close the hole and secure with a few stitches.

For all other sizes: continue.

Rows 34–36: Repeat Rows 2–4.

Row 37: [K2tog] 3 (4, 4) times, K0 (1, 0) [SSK]

Finished Circumference

32.5 (35, 40, 45, 49)cm or 13 (14, 16, 18, 19½)in
To fit up to 6 mths (6–12 mths, 12–18
mths, toddler to child, child to pre-teen)

Techniques

Cast on, cast off, knit, purl, cable work,
making a pompom, using markers,
3-needle cast off

Materials

Yarn

Debbie Bliss Rialto DK:
• 2 (2, 3, 3, 3) x 50g (1¾oz) balls Scarlet
  (012) – MC

Needles
• 4mm (US 6) needles
• 4mm (US 6) DPNS

Notions
• 2 stitch markers
• 4mm (US 6) cable needle

Construction

Knitted on two needles

Tension

22 sts and 30 rows to 10cm (4in) using
4mm (US 6) needles or correct size
needed to achieve this tension

Red Riding Hood

This pretty little hoodie is perfect for keeping snug and warm on long walks outside. It is bright and cheery and is sure to keep out the cold and the Big Bad Wolf.

Special Instructions

C4F: Cable 4 front as follows: slip next 2 stitches on to your cable needle, hold needle in front of your work, knit next 2 stitches from left-hand needle, then knit the 2 stitches off the cable needle.

C4B: Cable 4 back as follows: slip next two stitches on to your cable needle, hold the needle at the back of your work, knit next two stitches from left-hand needle, then knit the two stitches off the cable needle.

C3F: Cross 3 front as follows: slip next two sts on to your cable needle, hold needle at front of work, knit next st from left-hand needle then knit stitches from cable needle.

C3B: Cross 3 back as follows: slip next stitch on to cable needle, hold needle at back of work, knit next two stitches from left-hand needle then knit stitch from cable needle.

Instructions

Border

Using 4mm (US 6) needles, MC and cast on 94 (98, 110, 122, 130) sts.

Row 1: [K2, P2] to last 2 sts, K2.

Row 2: [P2, K2] to last 2 sts, P2.

Repeat rows 1 and 2 until work measures 2.5cm (1in).

Main Hat

Place markers where indicated (PM) and slip markers on subsequent rows where indicated (SM). Using markers makes it easier to keep track of where you are.

Row 1 (RS): K4, P4, C4F, P4, PM, K62, 66, 78, 90, 98, PM, P4, C4B, P4, K4.

Row 2: P4, K4, P4, K4, SM, P to next marker, SM, K4, P4, K4, P4.

Row 3: K4, P3, C3B, C3F, P3, SM, K to next marker, SM, P3, C3B, C3F, P3, K4.

Row 4: P4, K3, P6, K3, SM, P to next marker, SM, K3, P6, K3, P4.

Row 5: K4, P2, C3B, K2, C3F, P2, SM, K to next marker, SM, P2, C3B, K2, C3F, P2, K4.

Row 6: P4, K2, P8, K2, SM, P to next marker, SM, K2, P8, K2, P4.

Row 7: K4, P1, C3B, K4, C3F, P1, SM, K to next marker, SM, P1, C3B, K4, C3F, P1, K4.

Row 8: P4, K1, P10, K1, SM, P to next marker, SM, K1, P10, K1, P4.

Row 9: K4, P4, C4F, P4, SM, K to next marker, SM, P4, C4B, P4, K4.

Rows 10–16: Repeat Rows 2–8.

Repeat rows 9–16 1 (2, 3, 4, 4) more times.

For all sizes: Repeat Rows 9–12 once. Slip 47 (49, 55, 61, 65) sts to one DPN. Slip next 47 (49, 55, 61, 65) sts to second DPN. Fold work in half so RS are together and the WS is facing you. Work a 3-needle cast off. Weave loose ends into work and trim.

Scarf

Using US 6 (4mm) needles and MC, cast on 17 (19, 19, 21, 21) sts.

Row 1: [K1, P1] to the last st, K1.

Row 2: [P1, K1] to the last st, P1.

Repeat last 2 rows until scarf is approximately 100 (100, 100, 150, 150)cm, 40 (40, 40, 60, 60)in long (or if desired, continue until you have nearly used up your yarn, saving enough for two medium sized pompoms, see page 123). Cast off in rib pattern (either side of the scarf is the RS).

Making Up

Fold the scarf in half and mark centre with a pin. Place the hat seam to the centre scarf (with RS together) and stitch the hat edge to the scarf. Gather the cast-on edge of the scarf, pull tight and secure with a few sts. Gather the bound-off edge of the scarf tight and secure with a few sts. Make two medium sized pompoms (see page 123) and stitch to the gathered ends of the scarf.

Big Bad Wolf

Pair this hat with Red Riding Hood to make a classic duo of characters for a lot of play-acting fun.

Finished Circumference

32.5 (35, 40, 45, 49)cm or 13 (14, 16, 18, 19½)in
To fit up to 6 mths (6–12 mths, 12–18 mths, toddler to child, child to pre-teen)

Construction

Knitted flat on two needles

Techniques

Cast on, cast off, knit, purl, increase (YO, M1), decrease (K2tog, SSK)

Materials

Yarn

King Cole Baby Alpaca DK:
• 2 (2, 3, 3, 3) x 50g (1¾oz) balls Grey (502) – MC
• 1 x 50g (1¾oz) ball Charcoal (503) – CC

Needles

• 4mm (US 6) needles
• 4mm (US 6) DPNS
• 3.75 mm (US 5) needles

Notions

• Small square of washable black felt
• Scraps of washable light grey felt
• Black and grey sewing thread and needle
• Tape measure

Tension

22 sts and 28 rows to 10cm (4in) using US 6 (4mm) needles or correct size needed to achieve this tension

Instructions

Snout

Using 4mm (US 6) needles and CC, cast on 3 sts.

Row 1: K.
Row 2: P.
Row 3: K1, YO, K1, YO, K1. (5 sts)
Row 4: P1, P1tbl, P1, P1tbl, P1.
Row 5: K.
Row 6: P.
Row 7: K1, YO, K to last st, YO, K1. (7 sts)
Row 8: P1, P1tbl, P to last 2 sts, P1tbl, P1.
Rows 9–10: Repeat Rows 5 and 6.
Repeat rows 5–8 4 (4, 5, 6, 6) times until 15 (15, 17, 19, 19) sts are on needle finishing after a row 10.
Next row: K8 (8, 9, 10, 10) YO, K7 (7, 8, 9, 9). 16 (16, 18, 20, 20 sts)
Next row: P7 (7, 8, 9, 9) P1tbl, P8 (8, 9, 10, 10). Measure the length of the snout and make a note of it.

Border

Using 4mm (US 6) needles and MC, cast on 94 (98, 110, 122, 130) sts
Row 1: [K1, P1] to the end.
Row 2: [P1, K1] to the end.
Repeat rows 1 and 2 until work measures 2.5 (2.5, 3, 3, 3)cm, 1 (1, 1¼, 1¼, 1¼)in.

Main Hat

Work st st in MC until work measures the same length as the snout from the border cast-on edge.
Change to CC. Work 2 rows in st st.
Join the snout on the following row, using the three-needle knitting technique. When instructed, hold the snout stitches in front of the hat stitches with RS of snout facing out and knit both sets of stitches together.
Next Row: K39 (41, 46, 51, 55) join snout over the next 16 (16, 18, 20, 20) sts, K39 (41, 46, 51, 55).
Continue in st st until hat measures 11.25 (13.75, 16.25, 18.75, 18.75)cm, 4½ (5½, 6½, 7½, 7½)in.
Slip first 47 (49, 55, 61, 65) sts to one 4mm (US 6) DPN. Slip next 47 (49, 55, 61, 65) sts to second DPN. Fold work in half so that so that the RS are together and the WS are facing out. Using a 3rd DPN or 4mm (US 6)

needle, work a 3-needle cast off. Weave loose ends into work; trim.

Ears (make 2)

Use 3.75mm (US 5) straight needles and MC. Cast on 17 sts.

Row 1: K.

Row 2: P.

Row 3: K1, SSK, K to last 3 sts, K2tog, K1. (15 sts)

Rows 4–6: Starting with a P row, st st 3 rows.

Row 7: Repeat row 3. (13 sts)

Row 8: P.

Repeat last two rows four times. (5 sts)

Row 17: SSK, K1, K2tog. (3 sts)

Change to 4mm (US 6) needles and CC1.

Row 18: K.

Row 19: P.

Row 20: K1, M1R, K1, M1L, K1. (5 sts)

Row 21: P

Row 22: K1, M1R, K to last st, M1L, K1. (7 sts)

Row 23: P

Row 24: Rep Rows 22–23 three times. (13 sts)

Row 25: Rep Row 22. (15 sts)

Rows 26–28: Starting with a P row, st st 3 rows.

Rows 29–32: Repeat rows 25–28 once. (17 sts)

Cast off, then stitch the sloping sides of the ears together, leaving the straight edge open. The front of the ear is Gray (MC) and the back of the ear is Charcoal (CC).

Scarf

Using 4mm (US 6) needles and MC. Cast on 23 sts.

Row 1: [K1, P1] to the last st, K1.

Repeat Row 1 until your scarf is approximately 100 (100, 150, 150, 150)cm, 40 (40, 60, 60, 60)in long, or until you have used up your 2 balls of MC for the first 2 sizes or 3 balls of MC for the larger 3 sizes. You can use remaining balls of MC to make the scarf longer if you wish.

Making Up

Cut 4 small triangles of light grey felt slightly smaller than the knitted ear. Stitch 2 triangles together using whip stitch and white thread. Pin to the grey front of the ear and stitch in place. Pin the ears to the front of the hat, just above the snout, along the colour change line. Stitch ears in place with matching yarn.

Pockets

Note: For the 2 smallest sizes, omit the pockets and stitch the paw prints on to the scarf ends instead.

On a piece of paper, draw a wolf's paw print – that's a triangular shaped centre pad (with rounded edges) and 4 oval shapes to represent toes. Add a point to the top of each oval to represent claws. Cut out your paper template then use this to cut out 2 black felt paw prints.

Lay the scarf flat. Measure 15–18cm (6–7in) at each end of the scarf (long enough for a small hand). Place a pin to mark the measurement. Fold each end of the scarf up at the pin. Pin each paw print into place on the front of the upturned ends. Stitch into place with black sewing thread. Join

the sides of the pockets using MC and mattress stitch.

Fold the scarf in half and mark centre with a pin. Place the hat seam to the centre of the scarf (with RS together) and stitch the hat edge to the scarf.

Missy Mouse

Mice are popular in nursery rhymes, fairy tales and films. You can capture their cuteness with this sweet hat complete with fluffy pompom ears.

Finished Circumference

13 (14, 16, 18, 19½)in or 32.5 (35, 40, 45, 49)cm
To fit up to 6 mths/6–12 mths/12–18 mths/toddler to child/child to pre-teen

Construction

Knitted in the round

Techniques

Cast on, cast off, knit, purl, decrease (K2tog, PSSO, SSK), knitting in the round, knitting with DPNS, making a braided cord, making a pompom

Materials

Yarn

Sirdar Bonus DK:
- 1 x 100g (3½oz) ball Light Grey Mix (814) – MC

Sirdar Bonus Toytime DK:
- 1 x 25g (¾oz) ball Pink (992) – CC1
- 20cm (8in) length cream or white DK yarn – CC2
- 100cm (40in) length of black DK yarn – CC3

Needles

- 3.25mm (US 3) circular needles 40cm (16in)
- 4mm (US 6) circular needles 40cm (16in)
- 4mm (US 6) DPNS
- 4mm (US 6) needles for nose
- 3.75mm (US F, 5) crochet hook

Notions

Stitch marker

Tension

22 sts and 28 rows to 10cm (4in) using 4mm (US 6) needles or correct size needed to achieve this tension

Instructions

Border

Using 3.25mm (US 3) circular needles and MC, cast on 84 (90, 102, 114, 126) sts. Join the round and place marker. Work in garter st for 6 rows (in the round this is one row knit, one row purl, repeated). Change to 4mm (US 6) circular needles.

Start chevron pattern:

Round 1: [K1, M1L, K12 (13, 15, 17, 19) Sl2, K1, P2SSO, K12 (13, 15, 17, 19) M1R] 3 times.

Round 2: K. Repeat Rounds 1 and 2 until work measures 6 (8.5, 10, 13, 13)cm, 2½ (3¼, 4, 5, 5)in from beg (ending after round 2). Measure length at centre-front peak.

Decreasing

Round 1: K13 (14, 16, 18, 20) Sl2, K1, P2SSO, K25 (27, 31, 35, 39) Sl2, K1, P2SSO, K25 (27, 31, 35, 39) Sl2, K1, P2SSO, K12 (13, 15, 17, 19). (78, 84, 96, 108, 120) sts

Round 2 and every alternate round: K.

Round 3: K12 (13, 15, 17, 19) Sl2, K1, P2SSO, K23 (25, 29, 33, 37) Sl2, K1, P2SSO, K23 (25, 29, 33, 37) Sl2, K1, P2SSO, K11 (12, 14, 16, 18). 72 (78, 90, 102, 114) sts

Round 5: K11 (12, 14, 16, 18) Sl2, K1, P2SSO, K21 (23, 27, 31, 35) Sl2, K1, P2SSO, K21 (23, 27, 31, 35) Sl2, K1, P2SSO, K10 (11, 13, 15, 17). 66 (72, 84, 96, 108) sts

Round 7: K10 (11, 13, 15, 17) Sl2, K1, P2SSO, K19 (21, 25, 29, 33) Sl2, K1, P2SSO, K19 (21, 25, 29, 33) Sl2, K1, P2SSO, K9 (10, 12, 14, 16). 60 (66, 78, 90, 102) sts

Round 9: K9 (10, 12, 14, 16) Sl2, K1, P2SSO, K17 (19, 23, 27, 31) Sl2, K1, P2SSO, K17 (19, 23, 27, 31) Sl2, K1, P2SSO, 8 (9, 11, 13, 15). 54 (60, 72, 84, 96) sts

After round 10, change to 4mm (US 6) DPNS and start to decrease on every round as follows:

Round 11: K8 (9, 11, 13, 15) Sl2, K1, P2SSO, K15 (17, 21, 25, 29) Sl2, K1, P2SSO, K15 (17, 21, 25, 29) Sl2, K1, P2SSO, K7 (8, 10, 12, 14). 48 (54, 66, 78, 90) sts

Round 12: K7 (8, 10, 12, 14) Sl2, K1, P2SSO, K13 (15, 19, 23, 27) Sl2, K1, P2SSO, K13 (15, 19, 23, 27) Sl2, K1, P2SSO, K6 (7, 9, 11, 13). 42 (48, 60, 72, 84) sts

Round 13: K6 (7, 9, 11, 13) Sl2, K1, P2SSO, K11 (13, 17, 21, 25) Sl2, K1, P2SSO, K11 (13, 17, 21, 25) Sl2, K1, P2SSO, K5 (6, 8, 10, 12). 36 (42, 54, 66, 78) sts

Round 14: K5 (6, 8, 10, 12) Sl2, K1, P2SSO, K9 (11, 15, 19, 23) Sl2, K1, P2SSO, K9 (11, 15, 19, 23) Sl2, K1, P2SSO, K4 (5, 7, 9, 11). 30 (36, 48, 60, 72) sts

Round 15: K4 (5, 7, 9, 11) Sl2, K1, P2SSO, K7 (9, 13, 17, 21) Sl2, K1, P2SSO, K7 (9, 13, 17, 21) Sl2, K1, P2SSO, K3 (4, 6, 8, 10). 24 (30, 42, 54, 66) sts

Round 16: K3 (4, 6, 8, 10) Sl2, K1, P2SSO, K5 (7, 11, 15, 19) Sl2, K1, P2SSO, K5 (7, 11, 15, 19) Sl2, K1, P2SSO, K2 (3, 5, 7, 9). 18 (24, 36, 48, 60) sts

Round 17: K2 (3, 5, 7, 9) Sl2, K1, P2SSO, K3 (5, 9, 13, 17) Sl2, K1, P2SSO, K3 (5, 9, 13, 17) Sl2, K1, P2SSO, K1 (2, 4, 6, 8). 12 (18, 30, 42, 54) sts.

For 32.5cm, 13in size: cut yarn and thread on to a darning needle. Thread through remaining 12 sts, gather. Pull tight to close the hole; secure with a few stitches.

For all other sizes: continue.

Round 18: K2 (4, 6, 8) Sl2, K1, P2SSO, K3 (7,

11, 15) Sl2, K1, P2SSO, K3 (7, 11, 15) Sl2, K1, P2SSO, K1 (3, 5, 7). 12 (24, 36, 48) sts

For 35cm, 14in size: cut yarn and thread on to a darning needle. Thread through remaining 12 sts, gather. Pull tight to close the hole; secure with a few stitches.

For all other sizes: continue.

Round 19: K3 (5, 7) Sl2, K1, P2SSO, K5 (9, 13) Sl2, K1, P2SSO, K5 (9, 13) Sl2, K1, P2SSO, K2 (4, 6). 18 (30, 42) sts

Round 20: K2 (4, 6) Sl2, K1, P2SSO, K3 (7, 11) Sl2, K1, P2SSO, K3 (7, 11) Sl2, K1, P2SSO, K1 (3, 5). 12 (24, 36) sts

For 40cm, 16in size: cut yarn and thread on to a darning needle. Thread through remaining 12 sts, gather. Pull tight to close the hole and secure with a few stitches.

For all other sizes: continue.

Round 21: K3 (5) Sl2, K1, P2SSO, K5 (9) Sl2, K1, P2SSO, K5 (9) Sl2, K1, P2SSO, K2 (4). 18 (30) sts

Round 22: K2 (4), Sl2, K1, P2SSO, K3 (7), Sl2, K1, P2SSO, K3 (7), Sl2, K1, P2SSO, K1 (3). 12 (24) sts.

For 45cm, 18in size: cut yarn and thread on to a darning needle. Thread through remaining 12 sts, gather. Pull tight to close the hole; secure with a few stitches.

For 49cm, 19½in size: continue.

Round 23: K3, Sl2, K1, P2SSO, K5, Sl2, K1, P2SSO, K5, Sl2, K1, P2SSO, K2. (18 sts)

Round 24: K2, Sl2, K1, P2SSO, K3, Sl2, K1, P2SSO, K3, Sl2, K1, P2SSO, K1. (12 sts)

Cut yarn and thread on to a darning needle. Thread through remaining 12 sts to gather. Pull tight to close the hole; secure with a few stitches. Weave loose ends into work; trim.

Ears

With CC1, make two small pompoms (see page 123) and stitch one to each side of the top centre of the hat.

Nose

Using CC1 and 4mm (US 6) needles, cast on 10 sts (starting at the top of the nose).

Rows 1–2: Starting with a K row, st st 2 rows.

Row 3: K1, SSK, K to last 3 sts, K2tog, K1. (8 sts)

Row 4: P.

Rows 5–6: Repeat rows 3–4. (6 sts)

Row 7: K1, SSK, K2tog, k1. (4 sts)

Row 8: [P2tog] twice. (2 sts)

Row 9: K2tog. (1 st)

Cut yarn and pull through last st. Pull tight to fasten off. Stitch a straight line across the top of the nose in CC2, then stitch nose to centre-front face. Using CC3, stitch 3 long whiskers to each side of the nose, using the photo as a guide.

Braids

Cut 4 x 100cm (40in) lengths of CC1 and 8 x 100cm (40in) lengths of MC.

Using a crochet hook, pull 4 lengths of MC halfway through a stitch at the base of earflap point. Pull 4 lengths of CC1 halfway through the next st along then pull the remaining 4 lengths of MC halfway through the next st along. You now have 8 pieces of yarn in each section. Secure the hat between your knees and braid the 3 sections of yarn together. Make a knot at the end to secure the braids. Trim ends.

Adult Missy Mouse

It is more fun with two! Make a matching hat and share the excitement with another little mouse you know.

Finished Circumference
55cm, 22in
To fit an adult

Construction
Knitted in the round

Techniques
Cast on, cast off, knit, purl, decrease (K2tog, PSSO, SSK), knitting in the round, knitting with DPNS, making a braided cord, making a pompom

Materials
Yarn
Sirdar Bonus DK:
• 1 x 100g (3½oz) ball Light Grey Mix (814) – MC
Sirdar Bonus Toytime DK:
• 1 x 25g (¾oz) ball Pink (992) – CC1
• Short 20cm (8in) length of cream or white DK yarn – CC2
• 100cm (40in) length of black DK yarn – CC3

Needles
• 3.25mm (US 3) circular needles 40cm (16in)
• 4mm (US 6) circular needles 40cm (16in)
• 4mm (US 6) DPNS
• 4mm (US 6) needles for nose
• 3.75mm (US F, 5) crochet hook

Notions
Stitch marker

Tension
22 sts and 28 rows to 10cm (4in) using 4mm (US 6) needles or correct size needed to achieve this tension

Instructions
Border
Using 3.25mm (US 3) circular needles and MC, cast on 138 sts. Join the round ready to start knitting and place marker. Work in garter st for 8 rows (in the round this is one row knit, one row purl, repeated). Change to 4mm (US 6) circular needles.
Start chevron pattern:
Round 1: [K1, M1L, K21, Sl2, K1, P2SSO, K21, M1R] 3 times.
Round 2: K. Repeat Rounds 1 and 2 until work measures 13cm (5in) from beginning (ending after Round 2). Measure length at centre-front peak.

Decreasing
Round 1: K22, Sl2, K1, P2SSO, K43, Sl2, K1, P2SSO, K43, Sl2, K1, P2SSO, K21. (132 sts)
Round 2 and every alternate round: K.
Round 3: K21, Sl2, K1, P2SSO, K41, Sl2, K1, P2SSO, K41, Sl2, K1, P2SSO, K20. (126 sts)
Round 5: K20, Sl2, K1, P2SSO, K39, Sl2, K1, P2SSO, K39, Sl2, K1, P2SSO, K19. (120 sts)
Round 7: K19, Sl2, K1, P2SSO, K37, Sl2, K1, P2SSO, K37, Sl2, K1, P2SSO, K18. (114 sts)
Round 9: K18, Sl2, K1, P2SSO, K35, Sl2, K1, P2SSO, K35, Sl2, K1, P2SSO, K17. (108 sts)
After Round 10, change to 4mm (US 6) DPNS and start to decrease on every round as follows:
Round 11: K17, Sl2, K1, P2SSO, K33, Sl2, K1, P2SSO, K33, Sl2, K1, P2SSO, K16. (102 sts)
Round 12: K16, Sl2, K1, P2SSO, K31, Sl2, K1, P2SSO, K31, Sl2, K1, P2SSO, K15. (96 sts)
Round 13: K15, Sl2, K1, P2SSO, K29, Sl2, K1, P2SSO, K29, Sl2, K1, P2SSO, K14. (90 sts)

Round 14: K14, Sl2, K1, P2SSO, K27, Sl2, K1, P2SSO, K27, Sl2, K1, P2SSO, K13. (84 sts)
Round 15: K13, Sl2, K1, P2SSO, K25, Sl2, K1, P2SSO, K25, Sl2, K1, P2SSO, K12. (78 sts)
Round 16: K12, Sl2, K1, P2SSO, K23, Sl2, K1, P2SSO, K23, Sl2, K1, P2SSO, K11. (72 sts)
Round 17: K11, Sl2, K1, P2SSO, K21, Sl2, K1, P2SSO, K21, Sl2, K1, P2SSO, K10. (66 sts)
Round 18: K10, Sl2, K1, P2SSO, K19, Sl2, K1, P2SSO, K19, Sl2, K1, P2SSO, K9. (60 sts)
Round 19: K9, Sl2, K1, P2SSO, K17, Sl2, K1, P2SSO, K17, Sl2, K1, P2SSO, K8. (54 sts)
Round 20: K8, Sl2, K1, P2SSO, K15, Sl2, K1, P2SSO, K15, Sl2, K1, P2SSO, K7. (48 sts)
Round 21: K7, Sl2, K1, P2SSO, K13, Sl2, K1, P2SSO, K13, Sl2, K1, P2SSO, K6. (42 sts)
Round 22: K6, Sl2, K1, P2SSO, K11, Sl2, K1, P2SSO, K11, Sl2, K1, P2SSO, K5. (36 sts)
Round 23: K5, Sl2, K1, P2SSO, K9, Sl2, K1, P2SSO, K9, Sl2, K1, P2SSO, K4. (30 sts)
Round 24: K4, Sl2, K1, P2SSO, K7, Sl2, K1, P2SSO, K7, Sl2, K1, P2SSO, K3. (24 sts)
Round 25: K3, Sl2, K1, P2SSO, K5, Sl2, K1, P2SSO, K5, Sl2, K1, P2SSO, K2. (18 sts)
Round 26: K2, Sl2, K1, P2SSO, K3, Sl2, K1, P2SSO, K3, Sl2, K1, P2SSO, K1. (12 sts).
Cut yarn, leaving a long tail end. Thread tail end on to darning needle; gather remaining 12 sts. Pull tight to close the hole, secure with a few sts. Weave ends into work and trim.

Ears
With CC1, make 2 medium-sized pompoms (see page 123). Stitch to top of hat.

Nose

Using CC1 and 4mm (US 6) needles, cast on 10 sts (starting at the top of the nose).

Rows 1–2: starting with a K row, st st 2 rows.

Row 3: K1, SSK, K to last 3 sts, K2tog, k1. (8 sts)

Row 4: P.

Rows 5–6: Repeat rows 3–4. (6 sts)

Row 7: K1, SSK, K2tog, K1. (4 sts)

Row 8: [P2tog] twice. (2 sts)

Row 9: K2tog. (1 st)

Cut yarn and pull through last st. Pull tight to fasten off. Stitch a straight line across the top of the nose in CC2, then stitch nose to centre-front face. Using CC3, stitch 3 long whiskers to each side of the nose, using the photo as a guide.

Braids

Cut 4 x 100cm (40in) lengths of CC1 and 8 x 100cm (40in) lengths of MC. Using a crochet hook, pull 4 lengths of MC halfway through a stitch at the base of earflap point. Pull 4 lengths of CC1 halfway through the next st along then pull the remaining 4 lengths of MC halfway through the next st along. You now have 8 pieces of yarn in each section. Secure the hat between your knees and braid the 3 sections of yarn together. Make a knot at the end to secure the braids. Trim ends.

Celebrate in style

Here are hats for all occasions from birthdays to Halloween and Christmas. There is a cute pumpkin or a cuddly reindeer with antlers and ears. Stand out in the cold with a snowman or celebrate a birthday with a yummy cupcake topped with an oversized cherry. For the more adventurous knitter, there is a festive Christmas tree topped with a bright star, and the beginner can try their needles on the instantly recognisable Father Christmas hat. Whatever project you choose from this varied selection, it is sure to be a favourite.

Reindeer

This fluffy hat is sure to be a big hit at Christmas. Why not knit a whole herd of them?

Finished Circumference

32.5 (35, 40, 45, 49)cm or 13 (14, 16, 18, 19½)in
To fit up to 6 mths (6–12 mths, 12–18 mths, toddler to child, child to pre-teen)

Construction

Knitted in the round

Techniques

Cast on, cast off, knit, purl, increase (M1) decrease (K2tog), knitting in the round, knitting with DPNS, picking up and knitting sts

Materials

Yarn
Sirdar Snowflake Chunky yarn:
• 1 (1, 2, 2, 2) x 50g (1¾oz) balls Teddie (634) – MC
Sirdar Bonus Toytime DK:
• 1 x 25g (¾oz) ball Chocolate (947) – CC

Needles
• 4mm (US 6) circular needles, 40cm (16in)
• 5mm (US 8) circular needles, 40cm (16in)
• Set of 4 or 5 5mm (US 8) DPNS
• 3.25mm (US 3) needles

Notions
• Stitch holder
• Scraps of washable brown and cream felt
• Brown and cream sewing thread and sewing needle
• Small amount of toy filling for antlers and muzzle
• Stitch marker

Tension

14 sts and 19 rows to 10cm (4in) using 5mm (US 8) needles or correct size needed to achieve this tension

Instructions

Border

Using 4mm (US 6) circular needles and MC, cast on 44 (48, 56, 64, 68) sts. Join in the round and place marker. Work K1, P1 rib for 3.75 (3.75, 5, 5, 5)cm, 1½ (1½, 2, 2, 2)in.

Main Hat

Change to 5mm (US 8) circular needles and continue in st st until hat measures 5.5 (8, 10.5, 13, 13)cm, 2¼ (3¼, 4¼, 5¼, 5¼)in from border cast-on.

Decreasing

For 32.5 (49)cm, 13 (19½)in sizes only: [K9, 15, K2tog] four times. 40 (64) sts
For all sizes:
Round 1: (K6, K2tog) to the end. 35 (42, 49, 56, 56) sts
Round 2 and every alternate round: K.
Round 3: [K5, K2tog] to the end. 30 (36, 42, 48, 48) sts
Round 5: [K4, K2tog] to the end. 25 (30, 35, 40, 40) sts
Round 7: [K3, K2tog] to the end. 20 (24, 28, 32, 32) sts
Round 9: [K2, K2tog] to the end. 15 (18, 21, 24, 24) sts
Round 11: [K1, K2tog] to the end. 10 (12, 14, 16, 16) sts
Round 13: [K2tog] to the end. 5 (6, 7, 8, 8) sts
Cut yarn leaving a long tail. Thread tail on to a darning needle, gather remaining sts. Pull tight and secure with a few stitches. Weave all loose ends into the inside of the hat and trim.

Muzzle

The muzzle is in 3 sizes – small, medium and large. Use the small size for 13 (14)in, 32.5 (35)cm sizes, medium size for 40cm (16in) size and large size for 45 (49)cm, 18 (19.5)in sizes.
Using CC and 3.25mm needles, cast on 14 (18, 22) sts. Work 6 (8, 10) rows in st st.
Next Row (RS): K all sts then pick up and K 4 (6, 8) sts along the left row edge, turn. 22 (30, 38) sts
Next Row: P all sts then pick up and K4 (6, 8) sts along the right row edge, turn.
Work 10 (12, 16) rows in st st. Cast off, leaving a long tail for stitching muzzle to face.

Pin the muzzle to the centre-front face, above the ribbed border. The cast-off edge is the bottom edge of the muzzle. Stitch in place using tail end, stuffing with toy filling as you sew.

Antlers (make 2)

The antlers are in 2 sizes – small and large. Use the small size for 32.5 (35)cm, 13 (14)in sizes and the large size for 40 (45, 49)cm, 16 (18, 19½)in sizes.
Using CC and 3.25mm (US 3) needles, cast on 12 (15) sts.
Work 8 (10) rows in st st.
Next Row: K1, M1R, K1, M1R, K2 (3) slip next 4 (5) sts on stitch holder, K1 (pulling yarn tight across the back), K1 (2) M1L, K1, M1L, K1. (12 (14) sts left on needle)
Starting with a P row, st st 15 (19) rows.
Next Row: K2tog to the end. 6 (7) sts
Cut yarn leaving a long tail end. Thread tail

stitch. Fill with toy filling then stitch the cast on sts horizontally to the long antler. Make a second antler then stitch each antler to the top of the hat, approximately 2.5cm (1in) apart.

Ears (make 2)

For all sizes: cast on 6 sts using MC and 5mm (US 6) straight needles.

Row 1 (RS): [KFB, K1, KFB] twice. (10 sts)

Row 2 and every alternate row: P.

Row 3: [KFB, K3, KFB] twice. (14 sts)

Row 5: [KFB, K5, KFB] twice. (18 sts)

Starting with a P row, st st 7 rows for 32.5 (35)cm, 13 (14)in sizes and 9 rows for 40 (45, 49)cm, 16 (18, 19.5)in sizes.

Next Row: [K2tog, K5, K2tog] twice. (14 sts)

Starting with a P row, st st 3 rows.

Next row: [K2tog, K3, K2tog] twice. (10 sts)

Starting with a P row, st st 1 row for 32.5 (35)cm, 13 (14)in sizes and 3 rows for 40 (45, 49)cm, 16 (18, 19.5)in sizes.

Next Row: [K2tog, K1, K2tog] twice. (6 sts)

Next Row: P.

Next Row: [K3tog] twice. (2 sts)

Cut yarn leaving a long tail end. Thread on to a darning needle and pull through the 2 remaining sts on needle. Pull tight to fasten off. Fold ear in half and stitch the side seam and cast-on edge (use slip stitch with WS together). Stitch each ear to the base of each antler, so that it sticks out vertically to the side.

Eyes

Cut out 4 x 2cm (¾in) circles of cream washable felt for the eyes then cut out 2 smaller ¼ in (0.75 cm) circles of brown washable felt for the pupils. Whip stitch each brown pupil to the centre of 2 beige eyes. Whip stitch the second cream circle of felt behind each eye, then slip stitch the eyes to the face above the muzzle.

Nostrils

Cut out 4 x ¼ in (0.75 cm) circles of cream washable felt (2 per nostril). Whip stitch 2 felt circles together with matching thread then slip stitch to the muzzle.

end on to a darning needle and gather the remaining 6 (7) sts. Pull tight and secure with a few stitches.

Slip 4 (5) sts from stitch holder to one needle and rejoin CC.

For small size only:

Next Row: K1, M1R, K2, M1L, K1. (6 sts)

For large size only:

Next Row: K1, M1R, K1, M1R, K2, M1L, K1. (8 sts)

For all other sizes: continue.

Next Row: Cast on 2 sts , P across all 8 (10) sts.

Next Row: Cast on 2 sts, K across all 10 (12) sts.

Starting with a P row, st st 9 (11) rows.

Next Row: K2tog to the end. 5 (6) sts

Cut yarn leaving a long tail. Thread tail on to a darning needle and gather the remaining sts. Pull tight and secure with a few stitches.

Make up antler by stitching the long antler seam from the top, down to the cast-on edge. Fill firmly and evenly with toy filling. Stitch the short antler seam from the top down to the cast on sts, using mattress

Finished Circumference

32.5 (35, 40, 45, 49)cm or 13 (14, 16, 18, 19½)in
To fit up to 6 mths (6–12 mths, 12–18 mths, toddler to child, child to pre-teen)

Construction

Knitted in the round

Techniques

Cast on, cast off, knit, purl, decrease (K2tog), increasing (KFB), knitting in the round, knitting with DPNS

Materials

Yarn

Artesano Superwash DK:
- 1 x 50g (1¾oz) ball White (0157) – MC
- 1 x 50g (1¾oz) ball Lime Green (6315) – CC1
- 1 x 50g (1¾oz) ball Black (SFN50) – CC2
- Scraps of orange DK yarn for nose – CC3

Note: You only need a small amount of CC1 for the scarf border, so if you prefer you can use scraps of any DK yarn in the same colour with the same tension

Needles

- 3.25mm (US 3) straight needles
- 4mm (US 6) circular needles, 40cm (16in)
- Set of 4 or 5 4mm (US 6) DPNS
- 3.5mm (US F, 5) crochet hook for scarf fringe

Notions

- Stitch marker
- 1 large button for scarf (use a circle of felt for children under 3)
- 2 medium black buttons for eyes (use felt for children under 3)
- Scraps of green felt for holly
- 1 medium red half round button for holly (use red felt for children under 3)
- Stitch marker

Tension

22 sts and 30 rows to 10cm (4in) using 4mm (US 6) needles or correct size needed to achieve this tension

Snowman

It is chilly outside! Protect little ears with a snowman hat. He loves the cold and he is sure to make you smile on snowy days.

Instructions

Scarf Border

Using CC1 and 3.25mm (US 3) needles, cast on 84 (90, 102, 112, 122) sts.
Work 10 (10, 14, 18, 18) rows garter stitch, in the following stripe sequence:
2 (2, 4, 6, 6) rows CC1.
2 rows MC.
2 rows CC1.
2 rows MC.
2 (2, 4, 6, 6) rows CC1.
Cast off 12 (12, 14, 14, 14) sts. 72 (78, 88, 98, 108) sts
Transfer stitches to 4mm (US 6) circular needles. Join in the round ready to start knitting. Place marker.
Note: Stitches may feel tight but this will ease as you continue to knit.

Main Hat

Join in MC and work in st st until hat measures 7 (8.75, 10, 12.5, 12.5)cm, 2¾ (3½, 4, 5, 5)in from the border cast on. Join CC2 (cut MC).
Work 8 (10, 12, 12, 12) rows in garter stitch (one row knit, one row purl, repeated).
Work in st st until hat measures 8.75 (11.25, 13.75, 16.25, 16.25)cm, 3½ (4½, 5 ½, 6½, 6½)in from border cast on.

Decreasing

For 35 (45, 49)cm, 14 (18, 19½)in sizes only:
[K11 (47, 25) K2tog] to the end. 72 (96, 104) sts
Transfer stitches evenly between 3 or 4 DPNS before starting the decrease rounds.

Use the spare DPN to start knitting.
Round 1: [K6, K2tog] to the end. 63 (63, 77, 84, 91) sts
Round 2 and every alternate round: K.
Round 3: [K5, K2tog] to the end. 54 (54, 66, 72, 78) sts
Round 5: [K4, K2tog] to the end. 45 (45, 55, 60, 65) sts
Round 7: [K3, K2tog] to the end. 36 (36, 44, 48, 52) sts
Round 9: [K2, K2tog] to the end. 27 (27, 33, 36, 39) sts
Round 11: [K1, K2tog] to the end. 18 (18, 22, 24, 26) sts
Round 13: [K2tog] to the end. 9 (9, 11, 12, 13) sts
Cut yarn leaving a long tail end. Thread on to a tapestry needle and gather the remaining sts. Pull tight to close the hole and secure with a few stitches. Weave all loose ends into the inside of the hat; trim.

Nose

Using CC3 and 3.25mm (US 3) straight needles, cast on 8 sts.
Row 1: K.
Row 2: P.
Row 3: K5, K2tog, K1. (7 sts)
Rows 4–6: Starting with a P row, st st 3 rows.
Row 7: K4, K2tog, K1. (6 sts)
Row 8 and every alternate row: P.
Row 9: K3, K2tog, K1. (5 sts)
Row 11: K2, K2tog, K1. (4 sts)
Row 13: K1, K2tog, K1. (3 sts)

Row 15: K2tog, K1 (2 sts)
Row 16: P2tog. (1 st). Cut yarn, leaving a long tail. Thread on to a tapestry needle and pull through the remaining st. Cast off.

Making Up

Stitch the nose to the centre-front face. Stitch two black button or felt eyes above the nose. Cut 4 small holly leaf shapes from green felt scraps. Hold two leaves together and whip stitch around the edges with sewing thread. Repeat for second leaf. Stitch the two leaves to the hat brim, just right of the centre. Stitch a small red button (or circle of felt) to the lower points of the leaves.

Using the crochet hook method, add a short fringe to the scarf using CC1. Stitch a large button (or felt circle) to the cast-off edge of the scarf, stitching through both thicknesses of the border edge.

Father Christmas

The elfin style of this hat is perfect to help you get into the Christmas spirit.

Finished Circumference

32.5 (35, 40, 45, 49)cm or 13 (14, 16, 18, 19½)in
To fit up to 6 mths (6–12 mths, 12–18 mths, toddler to child, child to pre-teen)

Construction

Knitted in the round

Techniques

Cast on, cast off, knit, purl, increase (M1) decrease (K2tog), knitting in the round, knitting with DPNS

Materials

Yarn
Sirdar Bonus DK:
• 1 x 100g (3½oz) ball Red (833) – MC
Sirdar Snowflake DK:
• 1 x 50g (1¾oz) ball Milky (630) – CC1
Sirdar Bonus Toytime DK:
• 1 x 25g (¾oz) ball White (961) – CC2

Needles
• 3.25mm (US 3) circular needles 40cm (16in)
• 4mm (US 6) circular needles, 40cm (16in)
• Set of 4 or 5 4mm (US 6) DPNS

Notions
• Stitch marker
• Red seed beads (do not use for children under 3),
• White and red sewing thread, needle
• Stitch marker

Tension

22 sts and 28 rows to 4 in (10cm) using 4mm (US 6) needles or correct size needed to achieve this tension

Instructions

Border
Using 3.25mm (US 3) circular needles and CC1, cast on 62 (68, 78, 88, 98) sts. Join in the round ready to start knitting. Place marker. Work K1, P1 rib for 4 (4, 5, 5, 6)cm, 1½ (1½, 2, 2, 2½)in.

Main Hat
Change to 4mm (US 6) circular needles and MC.
Next Round: [K6 (7, 8, 9, 10) M1] nine times, K7 (4, 5, 6, 7) M1, K1. 72 (78, 88, 98, 108) sts
Continue in st st until hat measures 8.5 (11, 13.5, 16, 16)cm, 3½ (4½, 5½, 6½, 6½)in from border cast on.

Decreasing
Transfer stitches evenly between 3 or 4 DPNS before starting the decrease rounds. Use the spare DPN to start knitting.
Round 1: [K10 (11, 9, 12, 10) K2tog] to the end. 66 (72, 80, 91, 99) sts
Rounds 2–6: Continuing in st st, work 5 rounds.
Round 7: [K9 (10, 8, 11, 9) K2tog] to the end. 60 (66, 72, 84, 90) sts
Rounds 8–12: Repeat Rounds 2–6.
Round 13: [K8 (9, 7, 10, 8) K2tog] to the end. 54 (60, 64, 77, 81) sts
Rounds 14–18: Repeat Rounds 2–6.
Round 19: [K7 (8, 6, 9, 7) K2tog] to the end. 48 (54, 56, 70, 72) sts
Rounds 20–24: Repeat Rounds 2–6.
Round 25: [K6 (7, 5, 8, 6) K2tog] to the end. 42 (48, 48, 63, 63) sts
Rounds 26–36: Continuing in st st, work 11 rounds.
Round 37: [K5 (6, 4, 7, 5) K2tog] to the end.

36 (42, 40, 56, 54) sts
Rounds 38–48: Repeat rounds 26–36.
Round 49: [K4 (5, 3, 6, 4) K2tog] to the end. 30 (36, 32, 49, 45) sts
Rounds 50–60: Repeat rounds 26–36.
Round 61: [K3 (4, 14, 5, 3) K2tog] to the end. 24 (30, 30, 42, 36) sts
Rounds 62–72: Repeat rounds 26–36.
Round 73: [K2 (3, 13, 4, 2) K2tog] to the end. 18 (24, 28, 35, 27) sts
Rounds 74–84: Repeat rounds 26–36.
Round 85: [K1 (2, 12, 3, 1) K2tog] to the end. 12 (18, 26, 28, 18) sts
For all sizes: continue in st st until the hat measures approximately 45cm (17¾in) from the cast-on edge (or longer if desired).
Next Round: [K2tog] to the end. 6 (9, 13, 14, 9) sts

For 16/18 in (40/45 cm) sizes only:
Next Round: K1/0, [K2tog] to the end. 6 (7) sts

For all sizes: cut yarn leaving a long tail end. Thread on to a darning needle and gather the remaining 6 (9, 6, 7, 9) sts. Pull tight and secure with a few stitches.

Making Up

Weave in and trim loose ends inside the hat. Make a large pompom (see page 123) using CC2. Attach pompom securely to the hat with matching yarn. If desired, stitch seed beads around the white border.

Finished Circumference

32.5 (35, 40, 45, 49)cm or 13 (14, 16, 18, 19½)in
To fit up to 6 mths (6–12 mths, 12–18
mths, toddler to child, child to pre-teen)

Construction

Knitted in the round

Techniques

Cast on, cast off, knit, purl, decrease
(K2tog, P2tog), increasing (KFB), knitting
in the round, knitting with DPNS

Materials

Yarn
Sirdar Bonus DK:
• 1 x 100g (3½oz) ball Emerald (916) – MC
Sirdar Bonus Toytime:
• 1 x 25g (¾oz) ball Chocolate (947) – CC

Needles
• 3.25mm (US 3) circular needles, 40cm (16in)
• 4mm (US 6) circular needles, 40cm (16in)
• Set of 4 or 5 4mm (US 6) DPNS

Notions
• Stitch marker
• Small felt balls or tiny pompoms in
  bright colours
• Yellow felt square for star and contrast
  sewing thread, needle
• Stitch marker
• Seed or bugle beads

Tension

22 sts and 28 rows to 10cm (4in)
using 4mm (US 6) needles or correct size
needed to achieve this tension

Christmas Tree

Oh Christmas tree, Oh Christmas tree, how lovely are your branches.

Special Instructions

Make picot (MP) as follows:

K next stitch. Turn work. Using a 2-needle cast on method, cast on 6 sts (7 sts intotal). K across these 7 sts. Turn work. K across 7 sts. Turn work. Cast off 6 sts, leaving 1 st on right needle with yarn at back. Bring yarn forward between the needles then slip the stitch purlwise from the right needle to the left. Turn work carefully. Yarn is at the back ready to work the next stitch as instructed.

Instructions

Border

Using CC and 3.25mm (US 3) circular needles, cast on 72 (80, 88, 96, 104) sts. Join the round ready to start knitting. Place marker. Work in [K2, P2] rib until hat measures 2.5 (2.5, 5, 5, 5)cm, 1 (1, 2, 2, 2)in from border cast on. Change to MC and 4mm (US 6) circular needles and continue:
Next round: [K17 (9, 10, 11, 12) KFB] to the end. 76 (88, 96, 104, 112) sts

Main Hat

Round 1: [K1, MP] to the end.
Rounds 2–8: P 7 rows.
Round 9: [K2, MP] to the last 1 (1, 0, 2, 1) sts, K1 (1, 0, 1, 1). **For 45cm, 18in size:** MP on remaining st.
Round 10: [K17 (20, 22, 24, 26) K2tog] 4 times. 72 (84, 92, 100, 108) sts
Rounds 11–17: P 7 rows.
Round 18: [MP, K2] to the last 0 (0, 2, 1, 0)

sts, K0 (0, 0, 1, 0). **For 40cm, 16in size:** MP, K1 on remaining 2 sts, for 32.5cm, 13in size:
Go to 'Decreasing'. **For all other sizes:** continue.
Round 19: [K19 (21, 23, 25) K2tog] 4 times. 80 (88, 96, 104) sts
Rounds 22–28: P 7 rounds.
Round 29: [K2, MP] to the last 2 (1, 0, 2) sts, K0 (1, 0, 0). **For 35 (49)cm, 14 (19½)in sizes:** K1, MP on remaining 2 sts.
For 35 (40)cm, 14 (16)in sizes: go to 'Decreasing'.
For 35 (49)cm, 18 (19½)in sizes: continue.
Round 30: K.
Rounds 31–37: P 7 rounds.
Round 38: [MP, K2] to the last 0 (2) sts, K0 (0). **For 49cm, 19½in size:** MP, K1 on remaining 2 sts.

Decreasing

Transfer stitches evenly between 3 or 4 4mm (US 6) DPNS before starting the decrease rounds. Use the spare DPN to start knitting.
Round 1: [K6, K2tog] to the end. 63 (70, 77, 84, 91) sts
Rounds 2–8: P 7 rounds.
Round 9: [K2, MP] to the last 0 (1, 2, 0, 1) sts, K0 (1, 0, 0, 1). **For 40cm (16in) size:** K1, MP on remaining 2 sts.
Round 10: [K5, K2tog] to the end. 54 (60, 66, 72, 78) sts
Round 11: P.
Round 12: [P4, P2tog] to the end. 45 (50, 55,

60, 65) sts
Round 13: P.
Round 14: [P3, P2tog] to the end. 36 (40, 44, 48, 52) sts
Round 15: [P2, P2tog] to the end. 27 (30, 33, 36, 39) sts
Round 16: [P1, P2tog] to the end. 18 (20, 22, 24, 26) sts
Round 17: [P2tog] to the end. 9 (10, 11, 12, 13) sts
Cut yarn leaving a long tail end. Thread on to a tapestry needle and gather the remaining 9 (10, 11, 12, 13) sts. Pull tight and secure with a few stitches. Tie off and trim all loose ends of yarn inside the hat.

Embellishments

Decorations

Use felt balls as tree decorations or make small pompoms (see page 123). Stitch these over the hat using the sewing needle and thread.

Felt Star

Cut out a star shape from paper or card stock to your chosen size. Use this template to cut out 2 star pieces from yellow felt. Stitch seed beads or bugle beads to one side of each felt shape. Place the two star shapes together (beads on the outside) and whip stitch or back stitch the pieces together. Stitch to the top of the hat.

Finished Circumference

32.5 (35, 40, 45, 49)cm or 13 (14, 16, 18, 19½)in
To fit up to 6 mths (6–12 mths, 12–18 mths,
toddler to child, child to pre-teen)

Construction

Knitted in the round

Techniques

Cast on, cast off, knit, purl, increase (YO),
decrease (K2tog, SSK, K3tog), i-cord,
knitting in the round, knitting with DPNS,
pick up and knit stitches, purl through back
of loop

Materials

Yarn

Debbie Bliss Baby Cashmerino:
• 1 x 50g (1¾oz) ball Apricot (063) – MC
• 1 x 50g (1¾oz) ball Basil (061) – CC

Needles

• 2.75mm (US 2) needles for 32.5 (35)cm,
  13 (14)in sizes only
• 3.25mm (US 3) needles for 40 (45, 49)cm,
  16 (18, 19½)in sizes only
• 3.25mm (US 3) circular needles, 40cm (16in)
• 3.25mm (US 3) DPNS

Notions

• Stitch marker

Tension

25 sts and 34 rows to 10cm (4in) using
3.25mm (US 3) needles or correct size
needed to achieve this tension

Pumpkin

What's that moving in the pumpkin patch? It is an adorable autumn hat looking sweet as pie.

Instructions

Border

Using 2.75mm (US 2) needles for 32.5 (35) cm, 13 (14)in sizes and using 3.25mm (US 3) needles for 40 (45, 49)cm, 16 (18, 19.5)in sizes. With CC, cast on 6 sts.

Row 1: K3, YO, K to end. (7 sts)
Row 2: K3, P1, K3.
Row 3: As Row 1. (8 sts)
Row 4: K4, P1, K3.
Row 5: As Row 1. (9 sts)
Row 6: K5, P1, K3.
Row 7: As Row 1. (10 sts)
Row 8: K6, P1, K3.
Row 9: As Row 1. (11 sts)
Row 10: Cast off 5 sts, K1, P1, K3. (6 sts)

Rep Rows 1–10 until straight edge measures 32.5 (35, 40, 45, 49)cm, 13 (14, 16, 18, 19½)in when it is slightly stretched. Cast off all sts. Cut yarn, leaving a long tail; pull through last st. Stitch the cast-on and bound-off ends together.

Main Hat

Using MC and 3.25mm (US 3) circular needles. With RS of border facing, starting at the border seam, pick up and K78 (84, 96, 108, 120) sts across the straight edge. Join the round ready to start knitting. Place marker.

Round 1: [K4, P2] to the end.

Repeat Round 1 until the hat measures 9 (11.75, 14.25, 16.75, 16.75)cm, 3¾ (4¾, 5¾, 6¾, 6¾)in, from zig-zag edge of border.

Decreasing

Change to 3.25mm (US 3) DPNS for decreasing.

Round 1: [K4, P2tog] to the end. 65 (70, 80, 90, 100) sts
Rounds 2–4: [K4, P1] to the end.
Round 5: [K3, K2tog] to the end. 52 (56, 64, 72, 80) sts
Round 6: K.
Round 7: [K2, K2tog] to the end. 39 (42, 48, 54, 60) sts
Round 8: K.
Round 9: [K1, K2tog] to the end. 26 (28, 32, 36, 40) sts
Round 10: [K2tog] to the end. 13 (14, 16, 18, 20) sts
Round 11: K1 (0, 0, 0, 0) [K2tog] to the end. 7 (7, 8, 9, 10) sts

Stalk

Change to CC. Continue to knit in the round until stalk measures 4cm (1½in) or longer if desired. Cut yarn leaving a long tail. Thread on to a tapestry needle, gather remaining 7 (7, 8, 9, 10) sts. Pull tight, secure with sts. Weave ends into inside of hat and trim.

First Leaf

Note: The leaves use the YO increase method. Remember to purl into the back of the new stitch on each of the rows following the increase. This twists the stitch and avoids making a hole. Using CC, cast 3 sts on to one 3.25mm (US 3) DPN. Pick up and K 3 sts from the base of the stalk (6 sts). Purl one row, then work leaf as follows:

Row 1 (RS): [K1, YO, K1, YO, K1] twice. (10 sts)
Row 2: [P1, Ptbl, P1, Ptbl, P1] twice.
Row 3: [K1, YO, K3, YO, K1] twice. (14 sts)
Row 24: [P1, Ptbl, P12, Ptbl, P1] twice.
Row 5: [K1, YO, K5, YO, K1] twice. (18 sts)
Row 6: [P1, Ptbl, P5, Ptbl, P1] twice.
Rows 7–10: Starting with a K row, st st 4 rows.
Row 11: [K1, SSK, K3, K2tog, K1] twice. (14 sts)
Rows 12–14: Starting with a P row, st st 3 rows.
Row 15: [K1, SSK, K1, K2tog, K1] twice. (10 sts)
Rows 16–18: Starting with a P row, st st 3 rows.
Row 19: [K1, K3tog, K1] twice. (6 sts)
Row 20: P.
Row 21: [K3tog] twice. (2 sts)

Cut yarn leaving a long tail end. Thread on to a tapestry needle and gather the remaining 2 sts. Pull tight and secure with a few stitches. Fold leaf in half and stitch the side seam using a mattress stitch with WS together.

Second Leaf

Pick up and K 3 sts from the opposite side of the stalk. Knit an i-cord for about 5cm (2in). Cast on 3 sts, then repeat all instructions from Rows 1 of the first leaf.

Third Leaf

Pick up and K 3 sts from remaining side of the stalk. Knit an i-cord for approximately 10cm (4in). Cast on 3 sts, tthen repeat all instructions from Rows 1 of the first leaf.

Making Up

Stitch second and third leaves in place around the hat, using the image as a guide. Tie off and trim all loose ends to the inside of the hat.

Birthday Cupcake

Knit this treat in no time. Topped with a pompom cherry, it is sweet and delicious.

Finished Circumference

32.5 (35, 40, 45, 49)cm or 13 (14, 16, 18, 19½)in
To fit up to 6 mths (6–12 mths, 12–18 mths, toddler to child, child to pre-teen)

Construction

Knitted in the round

Techniques

Cast on, cast off, knit, purl, decrease (K2tog, P2tog), increasing (KFB), knitting in the round, knitting with DPNS, making a pompom, making a twisted cord, single crochet, slip stitch

Knit Kit

Yarn

Debbie Bliss Rialto DK:
• 1 (1, 1, 2, 2) x 50g (1¾oz) balls Pink (042) – MC
• 1 x 50g (1¾oz) ball Chocolate (005) – CC1
• 1 x 50g (1¾oz) ball Scarlet (012) – CC2
Note: only a small amount of CC2 is needed for the pompom (you may prefer to use scraps of DK yarn in the same colour, with the same tension).

Needles

• 3.25mm (US 3) circular needles, 40cm (16in)
• 4mm (US 6) circular needles, 40cm (16in)
• Set of 4 or 5 4mm (US 6) DPNS
• 3.5mm (US E, 4) crochet hook

Notion

• Stitch marker
• Red seed beads to be used for 'sprinkles', optional

Tension

22 sts and 30 rows to 10cm (4in) using 4mm (US 6) needles or correct size needed to achieve this tension

Instructions

Border

Using CC1 and 3.25mm (US 3) circular needles, cast on 72 (80, 88, 96, 104) sts. Join the round ready to start knitting. Place marker. Work in [K2, P2] rib until hat measures 2.5 (2.5, 5, 5, 5)cm, 1 (1, 2, 2, 2)in from border cast on.
Next row: [K17 (9, 10, 11, 12) KFB] to the end. 76 (88, 96, 104, 112) sts

Main Hat

Change to MC and use US 6 (4mm) circular needles.
Round 1: K.
Round 2–9: P 8 round.
Round 10: K.
Round 11: [K17 (20, 22, 24, 26) K2tog] 4 times. 72 (84, 92, 100, 108) sts
Rounds 12–20: Repeat Rounds 2–10. **For 32.5cm, 13in size:** go to 'Decreasing'.
For all other sizes: continue.
Round 21: [K19 (21, 23, 25) K2tog] 4 times. 80 (88, 96, 104) sts
Rounds 22–30: Repeat Rounds 2–10. **For 35 (40)cm, 14 (16)in sizes:** go to 'Decreasing'.
For 45 (49)cm, 18 (19½)in sizes: continue.
Round 31: K.
Rounds 32–40: Rep Rounds 2–10.
Round 41: K.

Decreasing

Round 1: [K6, K2tog] to the end. 63 (70, 77, 84, 91) sts
Rounds 2–9: P 8 rounds.
Round 10: K.
Round 11: [K5, K2tog] to the end. 54 (60, 66, 72, 78) sts
Rounds 12–14: P.
Round 15: [P4, P2tog] to the end. 45 (50, 55, 60, 65) sts

Rounds 16–18: P.
Round 19: [P3, P2tog] to the end. 36 (40, 44, 48, 52) sts
Round 20: P.
Round 21: [P2, P2tog] to the end. 27 (30, 33, 36, 39) sts
Round 22: [P1, P2tog] to the end. 18 (20, 22, 24, 26) sts
Round 23: [P2tog] to the end. 9 (10, 11, 12, 13) sts
Cut yarn leaving a long tail. Thread on to a tapestry needle and gather the remaining 9 (10, 11, 12, 13) sts. Pull tight and secure with a few stitches. Tie off and trim all loose ends of yarn inside the hat.

Icing Trim (Crochet)

Special Stitch: Make Picot (MP)
Make 5 ch, sl st into second chain from hook, 1sc into each of the next 3 ch.
Using MC and 3.5mm (US E, 4) crochet hook. Locate the back centre stitch of 'Main Hat', Round 1. Make a slip knot on to hook and jointo centre back stitch with a slip stitch. Work around round 1 as follows: [MP, sl st into each of next 2 sts], rep to the end of round 1. Sl st into first ch of first picot, cut yarn and pull through stitch on hook. Weave yarn ends into hat and trim.

Cherry and Sprinkles

Make a pompom to your chosen size in CC3 and attach to the top centre of hat (page 123). Cut a 60cm (24in) length of CC1 (chocolate) and make a twisted cord (page 125). Use a large tapestry needle to thread cord up through the centre of the pompom and out of the top. Stitch the ends of the stalk to the inside of the hat. Trim. If desired, sew red bead 'sprinkles' to the hat.

Dressing up

These hats are perfect for dressing up. Your child can join a pirate crew, become a budding chef or take on a royal role. Lock your doors if the Vikings land, or watch your little sunflower grow or create your own dinosaur hood that is bound to become a much loved accessory. The hats vary in style, from beanies to berets, and different techniques are used to create all kinds of textures and shapes.

Finished Circumference

32.5 (35, 40, 45, 49)cm or 13 (14, 16, 18, 19½)in
To fit up to 6 mths (6–12 mths, 12–18 mths,
toddler to child, child to pre-teen)

Construction

Knitted in the round

Techniques

Cast on, cast off, knit, purl, increase (M1, KFB),
decrease (K2tog), knitting in the round,
knitting with DPNS, wrap and turn, making
a bobble

Materials

Yarn
Artesano Superwash DK:
• 1 x 50g (1¾oz) ball Cocoa (SFN33) – MC
• 1 x 50g (1¾oz) ball Grey (SFN41) – CC1
Sirdar Click DK:
• 1 x 50g (1¾oz) ball Shale (176) – CC2
Sirdar Funky Fur:
• 1 x 50g (1¾oz) ball Chocolate (548) – CC3

Note: you only need a small amount of
CC2 and CC3, so you could use scraps
of any DK or eyelash yarn in the same
colours, with the same gauge

Needles

• 3.25mm (US 3) needles
• 2.75mm (US 2) needles for 32.5 (35)cm, (13
(14)in size horns
• 3.25mm (US 3) DPNS or any small–medium
size you have available
• 3.25mm (US 3) circular needles, 40cm (16in)
• 4mm (US 6) circular needles, 40cm (16in)
• Set of 4 or 5 4mm (US 6) DPNS

Notions

• Toy filling
• Stitch marker

Tension

22 sts and 30 rows to 10cm (4in) using 4mm
(US 6) needles or correct size needed to
achieve this tension

Special Instructions

Make bobble (MB) as follows:

Knit several times into the same stitch as
follows: K1, YO, K1, YO, K1. (5 sts)
Turn, K5 sts, turn, K5 sts, turn, K5 sts.
Turn, K2tog, K1, K2tog. Lift second st over
the first to cast off, then pass third st over
the first to cast off. (1 st)

Wrap and turn (W&T) as follows:

On a knit row: With yarn at back, slip next
stitch purlwise from the left needle to
right. Bring yarn forward. Slip same stitch
from the right needle back to the left. Take
yarn between the two needles to the back
of work. Turn the work so that the purl side is
facing. Yarn is at front, ready to work next row.

On a purl row: With yarn at front, slip next
stitch purlwise from the left needle to the
right needle. Take yarn to the back. Slip the
stitch from the right needle back to the left
needle. Bring yarn forward between the two
needles to the front of work. Carefully turn
your work so that the knit side is facing.
Yarn is at back, ready to work next row.

Viking

The Vikings did not really have horns on their helmets, but they certainly would have wanted one of these!

Instructions

Border

Using 3.25mm (US 3) circular needles and CC1, cast on 71 (77, 87, 97, 105) sts. Join in the round ready to start knitting. Place marker.

Round 1: [K1, P1] to the last st, K1.

Round 2: [P1, K1] to the last st, P1.

Rounds 3–4: Repeat Rounds 1–2.

Round 5: Repeat Round 1.

Change to 4mm (US 6) needles.

Round 6: K.

Round 7: K15 (18, 15, 20, 24) [P1, K7] 5 (5, 7, 7, 7) times, P1, K15 (18, 15, 20, 24).

Rounds 8–9: Repeat Rounds 6–7.

Round 10: K.

Round 11: K19 (22, 19, 24, 28) [MB, K7] 4 (4, 6, 6, 6) times, MB, K19 (22, 19, 24, 28).

Rounds 12–17: Repeat Rounds 6–11.

For 32.5 (35)cm, 13 (14)in sizes: go to Round 24. **For all other sizes:** continue.

Rounds 18–23: Repeat Rounds 6–11.

Rounds 24–28: Repeat Rounds 1–5, increasing one stitch at the end of Round 28 by working KFB into the last st. 72 (78, 88, 98, 106) sts

Main Hat

Change to MC . Work in st st until hat measures 8 (10.5, 13, 15.5, 15.5)cm, 3¼ (4¼, 5¼, 6¼, 6¼)in from cast on.

Decreasing

For 32.5 (35, 40, 49)cm, 13 (14, 16, 19½)in sizes only: [K34 (76, 20, 104) K2tog] to the end 70 (77, 84, 105) sts

Transfer stitches evenly between 3 or 4 DPNS before starting the decrease rounds. Use the spare DPN to start knitting.

Round 1: [K5, K2tog] to the end. 60 (66, 72, 84, 90) sts

Round 2 and every alternate round: K.

Round 3: [K4, K2tog] to the end. 50 (55, 60, 70, 75) sts

Round 5: [K3, K2tog] to the end. 40 (44, 48, 56, 60) sts

Round 7: [K2, K2tog] to the end. 30 (33, 36, 42, 45) sts

Round 9: [K1, K2tog] to the end. 20 (22, 24, 28, 30) sts

Round 11: [K2tog] to the end. 10 (11, 12, 14, 15) sts

Cut yarn leaving a long tail end. Thread tail end on to a tapestry needle and gather the remaining sts. Pull tight and secure with a few stitches. Weave all loose ends of yarn into WS of hat and trim.

Horns

For 32.5 (35)cm, 13 (14)in sizes use 2.75mm (US 2) needles; for 40 (45, 49)cm, 16 (18, 19½)in sizes use 3.25mm (US 3) needles.

Using CC2 and chosen needles, cast on 28 sts.

Rows 1–8: Starting with a K row, work 8 rows in st st.

Row 9: K1, SSK, K to last 3 sts, K2tog, K1. (26 sts)

Rows 10–12: Starting with a P row, st st 3 rows.

Rows 13–20: Repeat Rows 9–12 twice. (22 sts)

Row 21: K17, W&T.

Row 22: P12, W&T.

Row 23: K11, W&T.

Row 24: P10, W&T.

Row 25: K9, W&T.

Row 26: P8, W&T.

Row 27: K7, W&T.

Row 28: P6, W&T.

Row 29: K to end.

Row 30: P to end.

Row 31: K1, M1R, K8, SSK, K2tog, K8, M1L, K1. (22 sts)

Row 32: P.

Rows 33–48: Rep Rows 31–32 eight times.

Row 49: K1, M1R, K6, [SSK] twice, [K2tog] twice, K6, M1L, K1. (20 sts)

Row 50 and every following alternate row: P.

Row 51: K1, M1R, K5, [SSK] twice, [K2tog] twice, K5, M1L, K1. (18 sts)

Row 53: K1, M1R, K4, [SSK] twice, [K2tog] twice, K4, M1L, K1. (16 sts)

Row 55: [SSK] four times, [K2tog] four times. (8 sts)

Row 57: [SSK] twice, [K2tog] twice. (4 sts)

Cut yarn leaving a long tail end. Thread tail end on to a tapestry needle and gather the remaining sts. Pull tight and secure with a few stitches. Use tail end to stitch the side seam using mattress stitch. Fill horn really firmly with toy filling. Use cast-on tail end to stitch the horn to the side of the hat, above the rivet brim.

Horn Edging

Using CC3 and 3.25mm (US 3) DPNS, cast on 4 sts. Knit an i-cord until it is long enough to wrap around the base of the horn. Cast off. Stitch the cast on and cast-off sts together and stitch to the base of the horn at the point where it is attached to the hat.

Pirate

Ahoy there! Landlubbers need not apply for this hat. Trusty sea dogs should come aboard for treasure hunts. The eye patch is optional. Yarrh, Matey!

Finished Circumference

32.5 (35, 40, 45, 49)cm or 13 (14, 16, 18, 19½)in
To fit up to 6mths (6–12 mths, 12–18 mths, toddler to child, child to pre-teen)

Materials

Yarn

Sirdar Bonus DK:
• 1 x 100g (3½oz) ball White (961) – MC
• 1 x 100g (3½oz) ball Classic Red (833) – CC1
Sirdar Toytime Bonus DK:
• 1 x 25g (¾oz) ball (965) Black – CC2

Needles

• 3.25mm (US 3) straight needles
• 4mm (US 6) circular needles, 40cm (16in)
• Set of 4 or 5 US 6 (4mm) DPNS

Notions

• Stitch marker
• Pins

Construction

Knitted in the round

Techniques

Cast on, cast off, knit, purl, decreasing (K2tog), increasing (KFB), knitting in the round, knitting with DPNS

Tension

22 sts and 30 rows to 10cm (4in) using 4mm (US 6) needles or correct size needed to achieve this tension

Instructions

Border

Worked on straight needles.

Using MC and 3.25mm (US 3) needles, cast on 68 (74, 84, 94, 104) sts.

Work 10 (10, 12, 12, 14) rows in garter stitch. Leave sts on needle and cut yarn leaving a tail end for weaving into work later.

Main Hat

Using MC and 4mm (US 6) circular needles, cast on 2 sts. K border sts from straight needle. Cast on 2 sts. 72 (78, 88, 98, 108) sts Join in the round ready to start knitting. Place marker. Work the main hat in st st in the following colour sequence:

8 rounds MC (White), 8 rounds CC1 (Red) repeated. Cut yarn after each colour change. Work in st st until 16 (24, 32, 40, 40) rounds of stripes have been worked from the start of the main hat (not including border).

For 35 (45, 49)cm, 14 (18, 19½)in sizes only:
Maintain 8-round colour sequence and continue:

Next Round: K.

Next Round: [K11 (47, 25) K2tog] to the end. 72 (96, 104) sts

Next Round: K.

Go to 'Decreasing'.

For 32.5 (40)cm, 13 (16)in sizes: K3 rounds. Go to 'Decreasing'.

Decreasing

Transfer stitches evenly between 3 or 4 DPNS before starting the decrease rounds. Use the spare DPN to start knitting.

Round 1: [K6, K2tog] to the end. 63 (63, 77, 84, 91) sts

Round 2 and every alternate round: K.

Round 3: [K5, K2tog] to the end. 54 (54, 66, 72, 78) sts

Round 5: [K4, K2tog] to the end. 45 (45, 55, 60, 65) sts

Round 7: [K3, K2tog] to the end. 36 (36, 44, 48, 52) sts

Round 9: [K2, K2tog] to the end. 27 (27, 33, 36, 39) sts

Round 11: [K1, K2tog] to the end. 18 (18, 22, 24, 26) sts

Round 13: [K2tog] to the end. 9 (9, 11, 12, 13) sts

Cut yarn leaving a long tail. Thread tail onto darning needle, gather the remaining sts. Pull tight, secure with a few stitches. Weave loose ends into the inside of the hat and trim.

Ties

Using 3.25mm (US 3) needles and MC, pick up and pick up and K6 (6, 7, 7, 7) sts along one open edge of the border.

Work in garter stitch for approximately 12.5 (12.5, 15, 15, 15)cm, 5 (5, 6, 6, 6)in.

Next Row: K2tog, K to end.

Next Row: K.

Repeat last 2 rows until 2 sts remain. Cut yarn leaving a long tail. Thread tail on to tapestry needle, gather the remaining sts. Pull tight, secure with a few stitches. Weave loose ends into the inside tie. Repeat all tie instructions for the opposite edge of the border. Wrap the ties around each other once to create a mock knot. Secure the knot with a couple of stitches in MC.

Eye Patch

The eye patch is made in two sizes – small and large. Make the small patch for the 32.5 (35)cm, 13 (14)in sizes and make the large patch for the 40 (45, 49)cm, 16 (18, 19½)in sizes.

Strap

Using CC2 and 3.25mm (US 3) needles, cast on 4 (4) sts. Work in garter st until strap measures 31 (33.75, 38.75, 43.75, 47.5)cm, 12½ (13½, 15½, 17½, 19)in.

Next Round (buttonhole): K1 (1) YO, K2tog, K1 (1).

Continue in garter st until strap measures 32.5 (35, 40, 45, 49)cm, 13 (14, 16, 18, 19½)in. Cast off.

Fold strap in half and mark centre with a pin. Working from the pin toward the left, count 16 (20) garter stitch ridges then place another pin. Using CC2 and 3.25mm (US 3) needles, pick up and K16 (20) sts evenly between the pins.

Row 1: P.

Row 2: K.

Row 3: P.

Shaping

Row 1: K1, SSK, K to last 3 sts, K2tog, K1. 14 (18) sts

Row 2: P.

Repeat Rows 1 and 2 until 4 (6) sts are left (finishing after a row 1).

Next Row (foldline): K.

Next Row: K1, KFB, K to last 2 sts, KFB, K1. 6 (8) sts

Next Row: P.

Repeat last 2 rows until 16 (20) sts are on needle (finishing after a P row).

Starting with a K row, st st 2 rows. Cast off knitwise. Fold the eye patch in half at the fold line. Stitch the side seams closed with mattress stitch and matching yarn. Slip stitch the bound-off sts to the strap, stretching the strap slightly as you sew. Attach a button to the cast-on edge of the strap. The eye patch is designed to be worn over the hat but can also be worn independently.

Crown

Turn someone into a king, queen, prince, or princess in this majestic crown.

Finished Circumference

32.5 (35, 40, 45, 49)cm or 13 (14, 16, 18, 19½)in
To fit up to 6 mths (6–12 mths, 12–18 mths, toddler to child, child to pre-teen)

Construction

Knitted in the round

Techniques

Cast on, cast off, knit, purl, increase (M1, KFB), decrease (K2tog, SSK), knitting in the round, knitting with DPNS, making a pompom

Materials

Yarn

Debbie Bliss Cashmerino DK:
• 1 (2, 2, 2, 2) x 50g (1¾oz) balls Red (004) – MC

Debbie Bliss Cashmerino Aran:
• 1 x 50g (1¾oz) ball Gold (034) – CC

Needles

• 4mm (US 6) circular needles, 40cm (16in)
• 4.5mm (US 7) circular needles
• 5mm (US 8) circular needle, 40cm (16in)
• Set of 4 or 5 4mm (US 6) DPNS

Notions

• Selection of medium and small buttons or sew-on acrylic jewels
• Sewing thread in yellow, needle
• Stitch marker
• Pins

Tension

22 sts and 30 rows to 10cm (4in) using 4mm (US 6) needles or correct size needed to achieve this tension

Instructions

Main Hat

Use MC and 4mm (US 6) circular needles. Cast on 72 (78, 88, 98, 108) sts. Join in the round ready to start knitting. Place marker. Work in st st until hat measures 11.5 (14, 19, 19)cm, 4½ (5½, 6½, 7½, 7½)in from border cast on.

Decreasing:

For 35 (45, 49)cm, 14 (18, 19½)in sizes:
[K11 (47, 25) K2tog] to the end. 72 (96, 104) sts
Transfer stitches evenly between 3 or 4 DPNS before starting the decrease rounds. Use the spare DPN to start knitting.
Round 1: [K6, K2tog] to the end. 63 (63, 77, 84, 91) sts
Round 2 and every alternate round: K.
Round 3: [K5, K2tog] to the end. 54 (54, 66, 72, 78) sts
Round 5: [K4, K2tog] to the end. 45 (45, 55, 60, 65) sts
Round 7: [K3, K2tog] to the end. 36 (36, 44, 48, 52) sts
Round 9: [K2, K2tog] to the end. 27 (27, 33, 36, 39) sts
Round 11: [K1, K2tog] to the end. 18 (18, 22, 24, 26) sts
Round 13: [K2tog] to the end. 9 (9, 11, 12, 13) sts
Cut yarn leaving a long tail end. Thread on to a tapestry needle and gather the remaining sts. Pull tight and secure with a few stitches. Weave all loose yarn ends into WS of work and trim.

Crown

Use CC and 5mm (US 8) circular needles. Cast on 60 (60, 72, 84, 84) sts. Join in the round ready to start knitting. Place marker. Work 8 (8, 10, 10, 10) rows in garter stitch (one row knit, one row purl on circular needles).

Points

Each point is worked across 12 sts.
Rows 1–4: K12, turn.
Row 5: K1, SSK, K to last 3 sts, K2tog, K1. (10 sts)
Rows 6–8: K10, turn.
Row 9: Repeat row 4. (8 sts)
Rows 10–12: K8, turn.
Row 13: Repeat row 4. (6 sts)
Row 14–16: K6, turn.
Row 17: K1, SSK, K2tog, K1. (4 sts)
Row 18–20: K4, turn.
Row 21: K1, K2tog, K1. (3 sts)
Row 22: K3, turn.
Row 23: K3tog. (1 st)
Cut yarn and pull through last stitch. Weave yarn end into work and trim. Rejoin yarn and repeat Rows 1–23 until all points have been worked. There are 5 (5, 6, 7, 7) points in total.

Making Up

Weave loose ends into work and trim. On RS of the main hat, measure 2.5cm (1in) from the cast-on edge and mark with pins all around the edge. Slide the crown over the hat (with WS of crown against RS of hat) and line up the cast-on edge of the crown with the pins. Pin crown in place then slip stitch the edge of the crown to the hat. Use MC and stitch loosely so as not to restrict the stretchiness of the hat. The visible 2.5cm (1in) edge of the main hat should roll up naturally. Slip stitch the rolled edge to the edge of the crown, covering up any visible stitches. Make a mini pompom (see page 123) in CC and attach to the centre top of the hat. Stitch buttons or sew on jewels to the crown points.

Finished Circumference

32.5 (35, 40, 45, 49)cm or 13 (14, 16, 18, 19½)in
To fit up to 6 mths (6–12 mths, 12–18 mths,
toddler to child, child to pre-teen)

Construction

Knitted in the round

Techniques

Cast on, cast off, knit, purl, decreasing (K2tog,
P2tog), increasing (KFB), knitting in the round,
DPNS knitting

Materials

Yarn

Sirdar Bonus DK:
• 1 x 100g (3½oz) ball Chocolate (947) – MC
• 1 x 100g (3½oz) ball Sunflower (978) – CC1

Sirdar Toytime Bonus DK:
• 1 x 25g (¾oz) ball Emerald (916) – CC2

Needles

• 3.25mm (US 3) circular needles, 40cm (16in)
• 3.25mm (US 3) DPNS
• 4mm (US 6) circular needles, 40cm (16in)
• Set of 4 or 5 4mm (US 6) DPNS

Notions

• Stitch marker
• Pins

Tension

22 sts and 28 rows to 10cm (4in) using
4mm (US 6) needles over st st, or correct
size needed to achieve this tension

Special Instructions

Moss Stitch:

[K1, P1] repeated

Make picot (MP) as follows:

K next stitch. Turn work. Using a 2-needle
cast on method, cast on 8 sts (9 sts in
total). K across these 9 sts. Turn work.
K across 9 sts. Turn work. Cast off 8 sts,
leaving 1 st on right needle with yarn at
back. Bring yarn forward between the
needles then slip the stitch purlwise from
the right needle to the left. Turn work
carefully. Yarn is at the back ready to work
the next stitch as instructed.

Sunflower

Bring a little sunshine to the colder winter months with this bright, 'blooming' hat.

Instructions

Border

Using CC2 and 3.25mm (US 3) circular needles, cast on 72 (78, 88, 98, 108) sts. Join in CC1. Place marker. Join for working in the round.

Row 1: [K1 in CC2, bring CC1 forward between the two needles, P1 with CC1, take CC1 back] to the end. Cut CC2. Continue in CC1.

Row 2: [K1, P1] to the end. Repeat Row 2 seven more times.

Petals

Change to 4mm (US 6) needles.

Round 1: [K1, MP] to the end.

Round 2: K.

Round 3: [MP, K1] to the end.

Round 4: K.

Rounds 5–6: Repeat Rounds 1–2.

Main Hat

Change to MC.

Round 1: K to last 2 sts, K2tog. 71 (77, 87, 97, 107) sts

Round 2: [K1, P1] to last st, K1.

Round 3: [P1, K1] to last st, P1. Repeat Rounds 2 and 3 until work measures 8 (10, 13, 15, 15)cm, 3¼ (4, 5¼, 6, 6)in from border cast on, ending after a row 3. Transfer stitches evenly between 3 or 4 DPNS before starting decrease rounds. Use spare DPN to start knitting.

Round 1: [Starting with a K stitch, moss st 11 (11, 11, 13, 11) P3tog] 5 (5, 6, 6, 7) times, starting with a K stitch, moss stitch 1 (7, 3, 1, 6). **For 49cm, 19½in size only:** K3tog. 61 (67, 75, 85, 91) sts

Round 2 and every alternate round: [P1, K1] to last st, P1.

Round 3: [Starting with a K stitch, moss st 9 (9, 9, 11, 9) P3tog] 5 (5, 6, 6, 7) times, starting with a K stitch, moss stitch 1 (7, 3, 1, 7). 51 (57, 63, 73, 77) sts

Round 5: [Starting with a K stitch, moss st 7 (7, 7, 9, 7) P3tog] 5 (5, 6, 6, 7) times, starting with a K stitch, moss stitch 1 (4, 0, 1, 4). **For 35 (40, 49)cm, 14 (16, 19½)in sizes:** K3tog. 41 (45, 49, 61, 61) sts

Round 7: [Starting with a K stitch, moss st 5 (5, 5, 7, 7) P3tog] 5 (5, 6, 6, 6) times, starting with a K stitch, moss stitch 1 (2, 1, 1, 1). **For 14 in, 32.5 cm size only:** K3tog. 31 (33, 37, 49, 49) sts

Round 9: [Starting with a K stitch, moss st 3 (3, 3, 5, 5) P3tog] 5 (5, 6, 6, 6) times, starting with a K stitch, moss stitch 1 (0, 1, 1, 1). **For 35cm, 14in size only:** K3tog. 21 (21, 25, 37, 37) sts.

Round 11: [Starting with a K stitch, moss st 1 (1, 1, 3, 3) P3tog] 5 (5, 6, 6, 6) times, K 1 (1, 1, 1). 11 (11, 13, 25, 25) sts

For 45 (49)cm, 18 (19½)in sizes only:

Next Round: [P1, K1] to last st, P1.

Next Round: [K1, P3tog] 6 times, K1. (13 sts).

For all sizes: cut yarn leaving a long tail end. Thread on to a tapestry needle and gather the remaining sts. Pull tight and secure with a few stitches. Weave all loose yarn ends into WS of work and trim.

Ties (Make 2)

Lie the hat flat. Mark with a pin where ribbed edge folds on both sides. About 1cm (½in) behind 1 pin point, pick up and pick up and K 4 sts, using 3.25mm (US 3) DPNS and CC2. Knit an i-cord for 20cm (8in) or longer. Now, work in rows:

Next row (RS): K1, [KFB] twice, K1. (6 sts)

Next row: P.

Leaf

Row 1 (RS): [K1, YO, K1, YO, K1] twice. (10 sts)

Row 2: [P1, P1tbl, P1, P1tbl, P1] twice.

Row 3: [K1, YO, K3, YO, K1] twice. (14 sts)

Row 4: [P1, P1tbl, P3, P1tbl, P1] twice.

Row 5: [K1, YO, K5, YO, K1] twice. (18 sts)

Row 6: [P1, P1tbl, P5, P1tbl, P1] twice.

Rows 7–10: Starting with a K row, st st 4 rows.

Row 11: [K1, SSK, K3, K2tog, K1] twice. (14 sts)

Rows 12–14: Starting with a P row, st st 3 rows.

Row 15: [K1, SSK, K1, K2tog, K1] twice. (10 sts)

Row 16–18: Starting with a P row, st st 3 rows.

Row 19: [K1, K3tog, K1] twice. (6 sts)

Row 20: P.

Row 21: [K3tog] twice. (2 sts)

Cut yarn leaving a long tail. Thread on to a tapestry needle and gather the remaining sts. Pull tight and fasten off. Fold petal in half, stitch side seam (use a mattress stitch).

Second Leaf

Using 3.25mm (US 3) DPNS and CC2, cast on 3 sts. Pick up and K 3 sts vertically along the i-cord, 8cm (3in) above the first leaf.

Next Row: P.

Next, repeat all instructions for Leaf.

Third Leaf

Using US3 (3.25 mm) DPNS and CC2, cast on 3 sts. Pick up and K 3 sts vertically along the i-cord, 8cm (3in) above the second leaf.

Next Row: P.

Repeat all instructions for Leaf. Repeat all of the instructions for the second tie and 3 leaves.

Chef

Get out your pots and pans! It is time to cook up a storm in this delightful chef's hat.

Finished Circumference

32.5 (35, 40, 45, 49)cm or 13 (14, 16, 18, 19½)in
To fit up to 6 mths (6–12 mths, 12–18 mths, toddler to child, child to pre-teen)

Construction

Knitted in the round

Techniques

Cast on, cast off, knit, purl, increase (M1, KFB), decrease (K2tog), knitting in the round, knitting with DPNS

Materials

Yarn

Artesano Superwash DK:
• 2 (2, 2, 3, 3) x 50g (1¾oz) ball White (0157) – MC

Needles

• 4mm (US 6) circular needles, 40cm (16in)
• 3.75mm (US 5) circular needles
• Set of 4 or 5 4mm (US 6) DPNS

Notions

• Stitch marker

Tension

22 sts and 30 rows to 10cm (4in) using 4mm (US 6) needles or correct size needed to achieve this tension

Instructions

Rib

Using 3.75mm (US 5) circular needles, cast on 72 (78, 88, 98, 108) sts. Join in the round ready to start knitting. Place marker.
Round 1: [K1tbl, P1] to the end.
Repeat Round 1 until rib measures 7.5 (10, 1.5, 15, 15)cm, 3 (4, 5, 6, 6)in.
For 35cm, 14in size only: [K39, M1] twice (80 sts)
For 45cm, 18in size only: [K47, K2tog] twice (96 sts)
For 49cm, 19.5in size only: [K25, K2tog] four times. (104 sts)

Hat Top

Change to 4mm (US 6) circular needles.
Round 1: [K7, KFB] to the end. 81 (90, 99, 108, 117) sts
Round 2 and every alternate round: K
Round 3: [K8, KFB] to the end. 90 (100, 110, 120, 130) sts
Round 5: [K9, KFB] to the end. 99 (110, 121, 132, 143) sts
Round 7: [K10, KFB] to the end. 108 (120, 132, 144, 156) sts
Round 9: [K11, KFB] to the end. 117 (130, 143, 156, 169) sts
Round 11: [K12, KFB] to the end. 126 (140, 154, 168, 182) sts
Round 13: [K13, KFB] to the end. 135 (150, 165, 180, 195) sts
Round 15: [K14, KFB] to the end. 144 (160, 176, 192, 208) sts
Round 17: [K15, KFB] to the end. 153 (170, 187, 204, 221) sts
Work 4 (6, 8, 12, 12) rounds in st st.

Decreasing

When decreasing, change to 4mm (US 6) DPNS when necessary.
Round 1: [K15, K2tog] to the end. 144 (160, 176, 192, 208) sts
Round 2 and every alternate round: K.
Round 3: [K14, K2tog] to the end. 135 (150, 165, 180, 195) sts
Round 5: [K13, K2tog] to the end. 126 (140, 154, 168, 182) sts
Round 7: [K12, K2tog] to the end. 117 (130, 143, 156, 169) sts
Round 9: [K11, K2tog] to the end. 108 (120, 132, 144, 156) sts
Round 11: [K10, K2tog] to the end. 99 (110, 121, 132, 143) sts
Round 13: [K9, K2tog] to the end. 90 (100, 110, 120, 130) sts
Round 15: [K8, K2tog] to the end. 81 (90, 99, 108, 117) sts.
Round 17: [K7, K2tog] to the end. 72 (80, 88, 96, 104) sts
Round 19: [K6, K2tog] to the end. 63 (70, 77, 84, 91) sts
Round 21: [K5, K2tog] to the end. 54 (60, 66, 72, 78) sts
Round 23: [K4, K2tog] to the end. 45 (50, 55, 60, 65) sts
Round 25: [K3, K2tog] to the end. 36 (40, 44, 48, 52) sts
Round 27: [K2, K2tog] to the end. 27 (30, 33, 36, 39) sts
Round 29: [K1, K2tog] to the end. 18 (20, 22, 24, 26) sts
Round 31: [K2tog] to the end. 9 (10, 11, 12, 13) sts
Cut yarn leaving a long tail. Thread tail on to a tapestry needle, gather remaining sts. Pull tight and secure with a few stitches. Weave ends into WS of work; trim.

Finished Circumference
40 (45, 49)cm or 16 (18, 19½)in
To fit 12–18 mths (toddler to child, child to pre-teen)

Construction
Knitted flat

Techniques
Cast on, cast off, knit, purl, decrease (K2tog, P2tog, SSK), picking up sts

Materials
Yarn
King Cole Smooth DK:
• 1 x 100g (3½oz) ball Moss (884) – MC
• 1 x 100g (3½oz) ball Purple (890) – CC

Needles
• 3.25mm (US 3) needles
• 4mm (US 6) needles
• 3.75mm (US 5) needles

Notions
• Medium button
• Sewing needles and thread
• 2 small stitch holders

Tension
22 sts and 30 rows to 10cm (4in) using 4mm (US 6) needles or correct size needed to achieve this tension

Dinosaur

Delight your biggest dinosaur fan with this easy-to-knit hood. They will have a roaring good time playing dressing up or running around outside.

Instructions

Using US 3 (3.25) mm and MC, cast on 114 (126, 144) sts.

Rows 1–16: K2, [P1, K1] to the end.

Row 17: K2, P1, K1, [P1, K3tog, P1, K1] to the last 2 sts, P1, K1. 78 (86, 98) sts

Row 18–32: K2, [P1, K1] to the end.

Row 33: K2, [P1, K1] three times, K62 (70, 82). Slip remaining 8 sts from left needle on to stitch holder 1.

Row 34: K1 (1, 1), P60 (68, 80) K1 (1, 1). Slip remaining 8 sts from left needle on to stitch holder 2. Change to 4mm (US 6) needles.

Row 35: K.

Row 36: K1, P60 (68, 80) K1.

Rows 37–74: Repeat Rows 35 and 36 until hood measures 17.5 (18.75, 20)cm, 7 (7½, 8)in from start of st st ending after a row 36.

Crown Shaping

Row 1: K41 (46, 53) SSK, turn.

Row 2: Sl1P, P20 (22, 24) P2tog, turn.

Row 3: Sl1K, K20 (22, 24) SSK, turn.

Row 4: Sl1P, P20 (22, 24) P2tog, turn.
Repeat Rows 3 and 4 until all stitches are worked off each side of centre stitches. 22 (24, 26) sts left on needle.

Face Edging

Row 1: With RS facing, slip 8 st from stitch holder 2 on to needle. Using 3.25mm (US 3) needles, pick up and K32 (38, 44) sts from RS of the hood, K22 (24, 26) sts from the centre needle, pick up and K32 (38, 44) sts from the left side of the hood, [P1, K1] 4 times across the remaining 8 sts from stitch holder 1. 102 (116, 130) sts.

Row 2–6: K2, [P1, K1] to the end. Cast off in rib pattern.

Crests

Crest 1:

Using 3.75mm (US 5) needles and CC held double, cast on 16 sts.

Rows 1–2: K.

Row 3: K1, K2tog, K to last 3 sts, K2tog, K1. (14 sts)

Row 4: K.

Repeat Rows 3 and 4 until 4 sts remain (finishing after Row 4). K2tog twice, turn, K2tog. Cut yarn and pull through last st on needle. Pull tight to fasten off. Weave yarn ends neatly into crest.

Crests 2 and 3:

Using 3.75mm (US 5) needles and CC held double, cast on 18 sts. Repeat all instructions for Crest 1.

Crest 4:

Using 3.75mm (US 5) needles and CC held double, cast on 20 sts. Repeat all instructions for Crest 1. Stitch Crest 1 to the top of the hat above the ribbed edge then stitch Crests 2, 3 and 4 evenly along the centre line of the hood to the base of the ribbed edge, using the image as a guide.

Lower Hood Edging

With RS facing, using 3.25mm (US 3) needles and CC held double, pick up. and K16 sts from RS of the cast-on edge, starting at the right edge.

Row 1: K.

Row 2: K1, K2tog, K to last 3 sts, K2tog, K1. (14 sts)

Row 3: K.

Repeat rows 2 and 3 until 4 sts remain (finishing after Row 3). K2tog twice, turn, K2tog. Cut yarn and pull through last st on needle. Pull tight to fasten off. Work 5 (6, 6) more points in the same way, spaced evenly along the cast-on edge. Weave loose ends into the hood; trim.

Chin Strap

The chin strap is worked from one side of the face ribbed edging. Using 3.25mm (US 3) needles and MC, pick up and K8 sts along the upper edge of one side seam.

Row 1: K.

Row 2: K3, bind off next 2 sts, K2. (6 sts)

Row 3: K3, cast on 2 sts, K3. (8 sts)

Row 4, 6 and 8: K.

Row 5: K1, K2tog, K2, K2tog, K1. (6 sts)

Row 7: K1, K2tog, K2tog, K1. (4 sts)

Row 9: K2tog, K2tog. (2 sts)

Row 10: K2tog. Cut yarn and pull through last st on needle. Pull tight, fasten off. Stitch button on to the opposite ribbed edge, corresponding with the buttonhole strap.

Cute creatures

Whether you knit them for your own children, grandchildren or for friends, these whimsical creatures will be worn with pride. Frame your baby's face with a sleepy owl hat or take a child to visit the farm in an adorable chick hat, complete with legs and feet. Whichever quirky character you choose, you can be sure they will be cherished for a long time.

Bumblebee

This bee hat is cute as can be! It is great for girls and boys and is quick to make. Perfect for buzzing around on chilly spring days.

Finished Circumference

32.5 (35, 40, 45, 49)cm or 13 (14, 16, 18, 19½)in
To fit up to 6 mths (6–12 mths, 12–18 mths, toddler to child, child to pre-teen)

Construction

Knitted in the round

Techniques

Cast on, cast off, knit, purl, increase (KFB, M1L, M1R), decrease (K2tog), knitting in the round, knitting with DPNS, making a braided cord, making an i-cord

Materials

Yarn

King Cole Merino Blend DK:
• 1 x 50g (1¾oz) ball Black (48) – MC
• 1 x 50g (1¾oz) ball Yellow (55) – CC

Needles

• 4mm (US 6) straight needles
• 4mm (US 6) circular needles, 40cm (16in)
• Set of 4 or 5 4mm (US 6) DPNS

Notions

• Stitch marker

Tension

22 sts and 28 rows to 10cm (4in) using 4mm (US 6) needles or correct size needed to achieve this tension

Instructions

Earflaps (make 2)

Using MC and 4mm (US 6) needles, cast on 5 sts.
Row 1: K.
Row 2: P.
Row 3: K1, M1L, K to last st, M1R, K1.
(7 sts)
Row 4: P.
Rows 5–16: Repeat Rows 3–4 six times. (19 sts)
Starting with a K row, work 8 (10, 12, 14, 14) rows in st st. Cut yarn and slide earflap to the bottom of the needle. Cast on 5 sts with MC and make second earflap as instructed above. Cut yarn and leave on needle.

Border

Note: When you knit across the earflap sts, you will need to swap the left needle to your right hand, then swap the needle back to your left hand to continue casting on.

Using MC, and 4mm (US 6) circular needles and the cable method, cast on 7 (8, 11, 13, 15) sts, K across 19 sts from one earflap, cast on 19 (23, 27, 33, 39) sts, K across 19 sts from remaining earflap, cast on 7 (8, 11, 13, 15) sts. 71 (77, 87, 97, 107) sts Join in the round ready to start knitting. Place marker.
Round 1: K27 (27, 30, 32, 34) [P1, K1] 8 (11, 13, 16, 19) times, P1, K27 (27, 30, 32, 34).

Round 2: K28 (28, 31, 33, 35) [P1, K1] 7 (10, 12, 15, 18) times, P1, K28 (28, 31, 33, 35).
Repeat Rounds 1–2 three more times and on the last round increase 1 stitch by KFB in the last st for all sizes. 72 (78, 88, 98, 108) sts

Main Hat

Work main hat in the following colour sequence:
[8 rounds CC, 8 rounds MC] repeated.
Work in st st until 24 (32, 40, 48, 48) rounds have been worked from (and including) border Round 1.
For 35(45, 49)cm, 14 (18, 19½)in sizes:

Maintain colour sequence; continue as follows:

Next Round: K.

Next Round: [K11 (47, 25) K2tog] to the end. 72 (96, 104) sts

Next Round: K.

Go to 'Decreasing'.

For 32.5 (40)cm, 13 (16)in sizes only: K3 rows. Go to 'Decreasing'.

Decreasing

Transfer stitches evenly between 3 or 4 DPNS before starting the decrease rounds. Use the spare DPN to start knitting. Maintain colour sequence and decrease as follows:

Round 1: [K6, K2tog] to the end. 63 (63, 77, 84, 91) sts

Round 2 and every alternate round: K.

Round 3: [K5, K2tog] to the end. 54 (54, 66, 72, 78) sts

Round 5: [K4, K2tog] to the end. 45 (45, 55, 60, 65) sts

Round 7: [K3, K2tog] to the end. 36 (36, 44, 48, 52) sts

Round 9: [K2, K2tog] to the end. 27 (27, 33, 36, 39) sts

Round 11: [K1, K2tog] to the end. 18 (18, 22, 24, 26) sts

Round 13: [K2tog] to the end. 9 (9, 11, 12, 13) sts

Cut yarn leaving a long tail end. Thread on to a tapestry needle and gather the remaining sts. Pull tight and secure with a few stitches. Weave all loose yarn ends into WS of work; trim.

Braids

Cut 4 x 100cm (40in) lengths of CC and 8 x 100cm (40in) lengths of MC. Using a crochet hook, pull 4 lengths of MC halfway through a stitch at the base of earflap 1. Pull 4 lengths of CC halfway through the next st along then pull the remaining 4 lengths of MC halfway through the next st along. You now have 8 pieces of yarn in each of the 3 sections. Secure the hat between your knees and braid or plait the 3 sections of yarn together. Make a knot at the end to secure the braids and trim ends straight.

Antennae

Using MC and 4mm (US 6) DPNS, pick up and K 4 sts to the right of the centre point of the hat. Knit an i-cord for approximately 7.5cm (3in). Cut yarn leaving a long tail end. Thread on to a darning needle and gather the remaining sts. Pull tight and secure with a few stitches. Weave yarn end into antenna. Repeat for second antenna on the opposite side of the hat.

Ladybird

Stand out in the snow in this delightful hat. With its charming features it is sure to become a favourite and will keep your little one's ears toasty.

Finished Circumference

32.5 (35, 40, 45, 49)cm or 13 (14, 16, 18, 19.5)in
To fit up to 6 mths (6–12 mths, 12–18 mths, toddler to child, child to pre-teen)

Construction

Knitted in the round

Techniques

Cast on, cast off, knit, purl, increase (M1L, M1R), decrease (K2tog), knitting in the round, knitting with DPNS, short rows (wrap and turn), making a pompom, making an i-cord

Materials

Yarn

Debbie Bliss Cashmerino DK:
• 1 x 50g (1¾oz) ball Red (04) – MC
• 1 x 50g (1¾oz) ball Black (01) – CC

Needles

• 4mm (US 6) straight needles
• 4mm (US 6) circular needles, 40cm (16in)
• Set of 4 or 5 4mm (US 6) DPNS

Notions

• Scraps of black and white washable felt
• Black and white sewing thread and needle
• Stitch marker

Tension

22 sts and 30 rows to 10cm (4in) using 4mm (US 6) needles or correct size needed to achieve this tension

Special Instructions

Wrap and Turn (W&T):

On a knit row:

With yarn at back, slip next st purlwise from left needle to right. Bring yarn forward. Slip stitch from right needle back to left needle. Take yarn between two needles to back of work. Carefully turn work so purl side is facing. Yarn is at front, ready to work next row. **On a purl row:** with yarn at front, slip next stitch purlwise from the left needle to the right needle. Take yarn to the back. Slip the stitch from the right needle back to the left needle. Bring yarn forward between the two needles to the front of work. Carefully turn your work so that the knit side is facing. Yarn is at back, ready to work next row.

Instructions

Earflaps (make 2)

Using CC and 4mm (US 6) needles, cast on 5 sts.
Row 1: K.
Row 2: P.
Row 3: K1, M1L, K to last st, M1R, K1. (7 sts)
Row 4: P.
Rows 5–16: Repeat Rows 3–4 six times. (19 sts)
Starting with a K row, work 8 (10, 12, 14, 14) rows in st st. Cut yarn and slide earflap to bottom of needle. Cast on 5 sts with CC and make second earflap. Cut yarn leaving sts on needle.

Border

Note: When knitting across earflap sts, swap the left needle to your right hand then swap the needle back to your left hand to continue casting on.
With CC and 4mm (US 6) circular needles and the cable cast-on method, cast on 7 (8, 11, 13, 15) sts, K across 19 sts from one earflap, cast on 20 (24, 28, 34, 40) sts, K across 19 sts from remaining earflap, cast on 7 (8, 11, 13, 15) sts. 72 (78, 88, 98, 108) sts. Join in the round ready to start knitting. Place marker. Work 4 (6, 8, 10, 10) rows in st st.

Main Hat:

Change to MC and continue in st st until work measures 8 (10.5, 13, 15.5, 15.5)cm, 3¼ (4¼, 5¼, 6¼, 6¼)in from border cast on.
For 35 (45, 49)cm, 14 (18, 19½)in sizes:
Next round: [K11 (47, 25) K2tog] to the end. 72 (96, 104) sts

Decreasing

Transfer stitches evenly between 3 or 4 DPNS before starting the decrease rounds. Use the spare DPN to start knitting. Decrease as follows:
Round 1: [K6, K2tog] to the end. 63 (63, 77, 84, 91) sts
Round 2 and every alternate round: K.
Round 3: [K5, K2tog] to the end. 54 (54, 66, 72, 78) sts
Round 5: [K4, K2tog] to the end. 45 (45, 55, 60, 65) sts
Round 7: [K3, K2tog] to the end. 36 (36, 44, 48, 52) sts
Round 9: [K2, K2tog] to the end. 27 (27, 33, 36, 39) sts
Round 11: [K1, K2tog] to the end. 18 (18, 22, 24, 26) sts
Round 13: [K2tog] to the end. 9 (9, 11, 12, 13) sts
Cut yarn leaving a long tail end. Thread on to a tapestry needle and gather the remaining sts. Pull tight and secure with a few stitches. Weave all loose yarn ends into WS of work and trim.

Brim and Face

Using CC and 4mm (US 6) needles, pick up and K18 (22, 26, 32, 38) sts evenly along the centre-front edge, between the two earflaps. Starting with a P row, work 4 rows in st st.

Shaping

Row 1 (WS): Sl1, P16 (20, 24, 30, 36) W&T.
Row 2: K15 (19, 23, 29, 35) W&T.
Row 3: P14 (18, 22, 28, 34) W&T.
Row 4: K13 (17, 21, 27, 33) W&T.
Row 5: P12 (16, 20, 26, 32) W&T.
Row 6: K11 (15, 19, 25, 31) W&T.
Row 7: P10 (14, 18, 24, 30) W&T.
Repeat last 2 rows, following the set pattern, by working one stitch less before each W&T until you have worked the following row:
For 32.5cm, 13in size: P8, W&T.
For 35cm, 14in size: P8, W&T.
For 40cm, 16in size: P12, W&T.
For 45 (49)cm, 18 (19½)in sizes: P14, W&T.

For all sizes:
Next Row (fold line): P8 (8, 12, 14, 14) W&T.
Next Row: P8 (8, 12, 14, 14) K1, W&T.

Next Row: K9 (9, 13, 15, 15) P1, W&T.
Next Row: P10 (10, 14, 16, 16) K1, W&T.
Next Row: K11 (11, 15, 17, 17) P1, W&T.
Repeat last 2 rows, following the set pattern, by working one more stitch before the K1 or P1, W&T, until the following row has been worked: K15 (19, 23, 29, 35) P1, W&T
Next Row: P17 (21, 25, 31, 37).
Starting with a K row, work 4 rows in st st. Cast off knitwise. Slip stitch the bound-off edge to the first row of the brim.

Spots (Make 7)

Using CC and 4mm (US 6) needles, cast on 1 st.
Next Row: (K1, P1, K1, P1, K1) all into same stitch. (5 sts)
Next Row: P.
Next Row: K.
Next Row: P.
Next Row: K all sts, then lift second stitch over the first to cast off, lift third st over first to cast off, lift fourth st over first and fifth st over first (1 st left remains on needle). Cut yarn and pull through st. Tie the cast-on and bound-off tails together in a knot to create a bobble. Stitch each bobble to hat in a random pattern.

Antennae

Using CC and 4mm (US 6) DPNS, pick up and K 4 sts to the right of the centre point of the hat brim. Knit an i-cord until antenna is approximately 5cm (2in) long. Cut yarn leaving a long tail end. Thread on to a darning needle and gather the remaining sts. Pull tight and secure with a few stitches. Weave yarn end into antenna. Make a second antenna same of the first, For second antenna pick up and K4 stitches to the left of the centre point of the hat brim and repeat i-cord instructions.

Pompoms

Make 2 small pompoms (see page 123). Use the long ends from the knot to attach a pompom to the point of each ear flap.

Making Up

Fold the brim up towards the hat. Cut out felt circles for the eyes. Stitch pupils to eyes then stitch eyes to the brim and through the main hat to fix the brim to the hat. Tie off; weave loose ends into inside of hat and trim.

Finished Circumference

32.5 (35, 40, 45, 49)cm or 13 (14, 16, 18, 19½)in
To fit up to 6 mths (6–12 mths, 12–18 mths, toddler to child, child to pre-teen)

Construction

Knitted in the round

Techniques

Cast on, cast off, knit, purl, increase (M1, KFB), decrease (K2tog, SSK), making an i-cord

Materials

Yarn

Sirdar Bonus DK:
• 1 x 100g (3½oz) ball Bright Lemon (819) – MC
Sirdar Bonus Toytime DK:
• 1 x 25g (¾oz) ball in Bright Orange (981) – CC1
Scraps of red DK yarn – CC2
Note: The smallest 2 sizes use 25–30g (1–1¾oz) of MC, so you could use scraps of DK yarn with the same tension if preferred

Needles

• 3.25mm (US 3) DPNS
• 3.25mm (US 3) circular needles, 40cm (16in)
• 4mm (US 6) circular needles, 40cm (16in)
• 4mm (US 6) DPNS

Notions

• 2 x 1.5cm (½in) black felt circles
• 4 x 2.5cm (1in) white felt circles for eyes
• Stitch marker

Tension

22 sts and 30 rows to 10cm (4in) using 4mm (US 6) needles or correct size needed to achieve this tension

Chick

Chirp around the park in this adorable chick hat. Perfect for Easter or springtime fun.

Instructions

Earflaps (make 2)

The earflaps start with the i-cord foot:
* Using 3.25mm (US 3) DPNS and CC1, cast on 4 sts and knit an i-cord for 3cm (1¼in).
Next row: [K2tog] twice. (2 sts). Cut yarn. Leave i-cord on needle and put to one side.** Repeat from * to ** twice more. Do not cut yarn after third i-cord. Next, place the 3 i-cords on to one needle as follows: Hold needle with the first i-cord in your right hand. Slide the second i-cord onto same needle as the first i-cord so that it sits to the left of first i-cord; slide third i-cord (with yarn attached to ball) on to the same needle, so that it sits to the left of the second i-cord. (6 sts). Continuing in i-cord knitting, K1, K2tog, K2tog, K1. (4 sts). Continue to knit an i-cord on these 4 sts until foot measures 10 (10, 12.5, 15, 15)cm, 4 (4, 5, 6, 6)in.

Change to MC and start working in rows for the earflap:
Row 1: K2, M1L, K2. (5 sts)
Row 2: K.
Row 3: K1, KFB, K to last 2 sts, KFB, K1. (7 sts)
Rows 4–6: K 3 rows garter st.
Repeat Rows 3–6 until 15 (15, 17, 17, 19) sts are on needle.
Continue in garter st until work measures 5 (6.25, 6.75, 7.5, 8)cm, 2 (2½, 2¾, 3, 3¼)in from Row 1, finishing with RS facing. Cut yarn and leave sts on DPN. Repeat all instructions to make second ear flap.

Hat Border

Using 3.25mm (US 3) circular needle cast on 72 (78, 88, 98, 108) sts. Join the round ready to start knitting. Place marker. Join ear flaps on Round 1 below, using three-needle knitting technique. When instructed, arrange needles parallel to each other with earflap

stitches in front of cast-on stitches with RS of earflap facing out, knit both sets of sts together.
Round 1: K10 (11, 12, 15, 17) sts, join first earflap over the next 15 (15, 17, 17, 19) sts, K22 (26, 30, 34, 36) sts, join second earflap over the next 15 (15, 17, 17, 19) sts, K10 (11, 12, 15, 17) sts. 72 (78, 88, 98, 108) sts
Round 2: P.
Round 3: K.
Round 4: P.
Repeat last 2 rounds 3 (3, 4, 5, 5) more times.

Main Hat

Change to 4mm (US 6) needles. Work in st st in MC until hat measures 8 (10, 13, 15, 15)cm, 3¼ (4, 5¼, 6, 6)in from border cast on.

Decreasing

Transfer stitches evenly between 3 or 4 DPNS before starting the decrease round. Use spare DPN to start knitting.
For 35 (45, 49)cm, 14 (18, 19½)in sizes only: [K11 (47, 25) K2tog] to the end. 72 (96, 104 sts
Fr all sizes: continue.
Round 1: [K6, K2tog] to the end. 63 (63, 77, 84, 91) sts
Round 2 and every alternate round: K.
Round 3: [K5, K2tog] to the end. 54 (54, 66, 72, 78) sts
Round 5: [K4, K2tog] to the end. 45 (45, 55, 60, 65) sts
Round 7: [K3, K2tog] to the end. 36 (36, 44, 48, 52) sts
Round 9: [K2, K2tog] to the end. 27 (27, 33, 36, 39) sts
Round 11: [K1, K2tog] to the end. 18 (18, 22, 24, 26) sts
Round 13: [K2tog] to the end. 9 (9, 11, 12, 13) sts
Cut yarn leaving a long tail. Thread onto a tapestry needle, gather remaining sts.

Pull tight and secure with a few stitches. Weave loose ends into WS of work; trim.

Comb

Using CC2 and 4mm (US 6) needles cast on 8 (9, 10, 11, 11) sts using a two needle cast on method and work as follows:
* cast off until 1 st remains on right needle. Transfer this st back to the left needle and cast on 7 (8, 9, 10, 10) more sts using a two needle cast on method 8 (9, 10, 11, 11) sts ** Repeat from * to ** twice more. Cast off all sts. Cut yarn and pull through last st. Pull tight to fasten off. Stitch comb to centre top of head from front to back.

Beak

Using CC1 and 4mm (US 6) needles, cast on 14 sts.
Row 1: K.
Row 2: P.
Row 3: [K1, SSK, K1, K2tog, K1] twice. (10 sts)
Row 4: P.
Row 5: [SSK, K1, K2tog] twice. (6 sts)
Row 6: P.
Row 7: [Sl1, K2tog, PSSO] twice. (2 sts)
Cut yarn leaving a long tail end. Thread on to a darning needle and gather the 2 remaining sts. Pull tight and secure with a few stitches. Using mattress stitch, stitch the side of the beak closed. Stitch the open (cast on) edge to the top of the garter stitch border at the centre-front of the hat. Finally, add two eyes. Whip stitch each pupil to the centre of a white eye. Whip stitch the second white felt circle behind each eye, then slip stitch the eyes

Owl

He's a wise old owl who loves to fly around the woods or sit in a tall tree watching the world go by.

Finished Circumference

32.5 (35, 40, 45, 49)cm or 13 (14, 16, 18, 19½)in
To fit up to 6 mths/6–12 mths/12–18 mths/toddler to child/child to pre-teen

Construction

Knitted in the round

Techniques

Cast on, cast off, knit, purl, decrease (SSK, K2tog), knitting in the round

Materials

Yarn
Artesano Superwash DK:
• 1 x 50g (1¾oz) ball Shade 3068 Brown – MC
• 1 x 50g (1¾oz) ball Shade 5771 Baby Teal – CC1
• Orange DK yarn for beak and braids – CC2

Needles
• 3.75mm (US 5) DPNS
• 3.75mm (US 5) circular needles, 40cm (16in)
• 4mm (US 6) circular needles, 40cm (16in)
• set of 4 or 5 4mm (US 6) DPNS
• Medium crochet hook for attaching ear tufts

Notions
• Scraps of black washable felt for eyes
• Small square white and turquoise washable felt
• Black, white, turquoise thread and needle
• Stitch marker

Tension

22 sts and 30 rows to 10cm (4in) using 4mm (US 6) needles or correct size needed to achieve this tension

Instructions

Ear Flap (make 2)
Using 3.75mm (US 5) DPNS and MC, cast on 4 sts.
Row 1: K.
Row 2: K1, P to last st, K1.
Row 3: K1, [KFB] twice, K1. (6 sts)
Row 4: K1, P to last st, K1.
Row 5: K1, KFB, K to last 2 sts, KFB, K1. (8sts)
Row 6: Rep Row 4.
Repeat Rows 5 & 6 until 16 (16, 18, 18, 18) sts are on needle finishing after a Row 6.
Next Row: K.
Next Row: K1, P to last st, K1.
For sizes 45 (49)cm, 18 (19½)in only:
Repeat last 2 rows once more. Cut yarn and leave sts on needle. Make second ear flap.

Hat Border
Using MC and 3.75mm (US 5) circular needles, cast on 71 (75, 87, 95, 107) sts. Join the round ready to start knitting. Place marker. Join ear-flaps on Round 1 below, using the three-needle knitting technique. When instructed, arrange needles parallel to each other with earflap stitches in front of cast on stitches with RS of earflap facing; knit both sets of corresponding stitches together. Centre-front stitches to create a moss stitch border.
Round 1: K9 (9, 12, 13, 16), join first earflap over the next 16 (16, 18, 18, 18) sts, [P1, K1] 10 (12, 13, 16, 19) times, P1, join second earflap over the next 16 (16, 18, 18, 18) sts, K9 (9, 12, 13, 16). 71 (75, 87, 95, 107) sts
Round 2: K26 (26, 31, 33, 35) [P1, K1] 10 (12, 13, 16, 19) times K25 (25, 30, 32, 34).
Round 3: K25 (25, 30, 32, 34) [P1, K1] 10 (12, 13, 16, 19) times, P1, K25 (25, 30, 32, 34).
Round 4: As Round 2.
Repeat Rounds 3 and 4 once more and on the last round increase 1 stitch by KFB in the last st for all sizes. 72 (76, 88, 96, 108) sts

Main Hat
Change to 4mm (US 6) needles.
Work in st st until hat measures 6.25 (7.5, 8.75, 11.25, 11.25)cm, 2½ (3, 3½, 4½, 4½)in (from cast on edge. Cut CC1, change to MC.
Continue in st st until hat measures 11.25 (13.75, 16.25, 18.75, 18.75)cm, 4½ (5½, 6½, 7½, 7½)in from cast-on edge.
Cut yarn. Slip first 18 (19, 22, 24, 27) sts to first 4mm (US 6) DPN, slip next 36 (38, 44, 48, 54) sts to second DPN, slip remaining 18 (19, 22, 24, 27) sts to opposite end of first DPN. Turn hat inside out so WS faces you. Using MC, cast off the sts using three-needle cast off. Tie off; trim loose ends inside the hat. Alternatively, cast off all sts and stitch seam closed using mattress stitch.

Beak
Using CC2 and 3.75mm (US 5) needles, cast on 18 sts.
Row 1: K.
Row 2: P.
Row 3: [K1, SSK, K3, K2tog, K1] twice. (14 sts)
Rows 4–6: Starting with a P row, st st 3 rows.
Row 7: [K1, SSK, K1, K2tog, K1] twice. (10 sts)
Row 8–10: Starting with a P row, st st 3 rows.
Row 11: [K1, K3tog, K1] twice. (6 sts)
Row 12: P.
Row 13: [K3tog] twice. (2 sts)
Cut yarn leaving a long tail. Thread tail on to darning needle and cast off the 2 remaining sts. Pull tight to fasten off. Fold beak in half and stitch the side and top seams (use mattress stitch with WS together).

Eyes

Cut 4 circles of white washable felt approximately 6cm (2½in) across (a front and back for each eye). From turquoise washable felt, cut 1 smaller circle of felt approximately 4cm (1½in) across (or cut out a flower shape instead). From black washable felt, cut 1 small circle of felt approximately 2cm (¾in) across. On to one large white circle of felt, stitch a closed sleepy eye, using the hat image as a guide. This is the front of one eye. Stitch this front eye to back using white thread and whip stitch. To make second eye, stitch black pupil to centre of turquoise circle or flower. Next, stitch the turquoise circle

or flower to a large white circle using matching thread and whip stitch. Stitch the front eye to the back using white thread and whip stitch. Position eyes in place along the colour change line and pin your beak between the eyes just below the colour change line. Slip stitch into place using matching thread or yarn as appropriate.

Ear Tufts

Cut approximately 24 x 10cm (4in) strands of CC1 and use the crochet hook method to join 12 strips of yarn to each corner of hat.

Braids

Cut 3 x 100cm (40in) lengths of MC, 3 x 100cm (40in) lengths of CC1 and 3 x 100cm (40in) lengths of CC2. Using a crochet hook, pull 3 lengths of MC halfway through a stitch at the base of earflap 1. Pull 3 lengths of CC1 halfway through the next st along then pull 3 lengths of CC2 halfway through the next st along. You now have 6 pieces of yarn in each of the 3 sections. Secure the hat between your knees and braid or plait the 3 sections of yarn together. Make a knot at the end to secure the braids; trim ends.

Knitted monsters

These quirky characters are sure to brighten up cold and dull
days. The designs feature all sorts of customised techniques and finishing touches, such
as rolled brims and braided earflaps. Turn your little angel into a mischievous devil or
frighten friends with a bright green ogre hat. With a little imagination and a lot of
energy, any child will be able to invent games and create characters in these hats.

Mini One-Eye!

He has got his eye on you! Knit this amazing hat and you will get all the attention! Who can resist that goofy grin and spiky top?

Finished Circumference

32.5 (35, 40, 45, 49)cm or 13 (14, 16, 18, 19½)in
To fit up to 6 mths/6–12 mths/12–18 mths/
toddler to child/child to pre-teen

Note: Instructions are provided for both a crochet eye and a felt eye

Construction

Knitted in the round

Techniques

Cast on, cast off, knit, purl, increase (M1, KFB), decrease (K2tog, SSK), making a braid, optional crochet (dc in the round)

Materials

Yarn

Rowan All Seasons Cotton:
- 1 (1, 1, 2, 2) x 50g (1¾oz) balls Jacuzzi (239) – MC
- 1 (1, 1, 1, 1) x 50g (1¾oz) ball Lime (241) – CC1
- Scraps of Organic (178) or worsted weight cream yarn – CC2
- Scraps of black DK yarn – CC3

Needles

- 4.5mm (US 7) needles
- 3.75 or 4mm (US 5 or 6) needles
- 3.25mm (US 3) DPNS
- 4.5mm (US 7) circular needles, 40cm (16in)
- 5mm (US 8) circular needles, 40cm (16in)
- Set of 4 or 5 5mm (US 8) DPNS
- 4mm (US G,6) crochet hook

Notions

- Washable felt in turquoise, lime green, black and white for the eye
- For crochet eyes: 4mm (US G, 6) crochet hook and scraps of black washable felt
- Sewing thread in black, white, green and turquoise, needle
- White washable felt for teeth
- Stitch marker

Tension

16 sts and 23 rows to 10cm (4in) using 5mm (US 8) needles or correct size needed to achieve this tension

Instructions

Earflaps (make 2)

Using 4.5mm (US 7) needles and MC, cast on 4 sts for all sizes.

Row 1 (RS): K.

Row 2 (WS): K1, P to last st, K1.

Row 3: K1, [KFB] twice, K1. (6 sts)

Row 4: K1, P to last st, K1.

Row 5: K1, KFB, K to last 2 sts, KFB, K1. (8 sts)

Row 6: Repeat Row 4.

Repeat rows 5 and 6 until 16 (16, 16, 18, 18) sts are on the needle.

Next Row: K.

Next Row: K1, P to last st, K1.

For sizes 45 (49)cm, 18 (19½)in: repeat last 2 rows once more. Cut yarn and leave sts on needle. Repeat all instructions to make second earflap.

Hat Border

Using MC and 4.5mm (US 7) circular needles, cast on 53 (57, 65, 73, 79) sts. Join in the round ready to start knitting and place

marker for beginning of round.

Join the earflaps on Round 1 below, using the three-needle knitting technique. When instructed, arrange needles parallel to each other with earflap stitches in front of the cast-on stitches with RS of earflap facing you and knit both sets of corresponding stitches together. The centre-front stitches create a moss stitch border.

Round 1: K5, 5, 7, 8, 10 sts, join first earflap over the next 16, 16, 16, 18, 18 sts, [P1, K1] 5, 7, 9, 10, 11 times, P1, join second earflap over the next 16 (16, 16, 18, 18) sts, K5 (5, 7, 8, 10) sts. 53 (57, 65, 73, 79) sts

Round 2: K22 (22, 24, 27, 29) sts, [P1, K1] 5 (7, 9, 10, 11) times K20 (20, 22, 25, 27) KFB. 54 (58, 66, 74, 80) sts

Main Hat

Change to 5mm (US 8) using circular needles, join CC1 (do not cut MC) and work 2 rows of st st in CC1.

Cut CC1; continue working st st in MC until

hat measures 7.5 (10, 12.5, 15, 15)cm, 3 (4, 5, 6)in, from border cast on.

Decreasing

Transfer stitches evenly between 3 or 4 5mm (US 8) DPNS before starting the decrease rounds. Use the spare DPN to start knitting.

For 32.5 (35, 40, 45)cm, 13 (14, 16, 18)in sizes:

Next Round: [K7 (27, 31, 35) K2tog] to the end. 48 (56, 64, 72) sts

For all sizes your stitch count is now divisible by 8 for the decrease rounds. 48 (56, 64, 72, 80) sts.

Round 1: [K6, K2tog] to the end. 42 (49, 56, 63, 70) sts

Round 2 and every alternate round: K.

Round 3: [K5, K2tog] to the end. 36 (42, 48, 54, 60) sts

Round 5: [K4, K2tog] to the end. 30 (35, 40, 45, 50) sts

Round 7: [K3, K2tog] to the end. 24 (28, 32, 36, 40) sts

rows in st st.

Row 11: [K1, K3tog, K1] twice. (6 sts)

Row 12: [P3tog] twice. (2 sts). Cut yarn leaving a long tail end. Thread tail end on to a tapestry needle and gather the remaining sts. Pull tight and secure with a few sts. Fold spike in half and stitch all seams using mattress stitch with WS together.

For 32.5 (35, 40)cm, 13 (14, 16)in sizes: make 1 more spike in MC and 1 in CC1. **For 45 (49) cm, 18 (19½)in sizes:** make 1 more spike in MC and 3 in CC1.

Felt Eye

For 45 (49)cm, 18 (19½)in sizes:

Cut 5 circles of washable felt as follows:

2 x white measuring 7.5cm (3in) across.

1 x green measuring 5cm (2in) across.

1 x turquoise measuring 4cm (1½in) across.

1 x black measuring 2cm (¾in) across.

Stitch the black pupil to the centre of the turquoise circle. Stitch the turquoise circle to the centre of the green circle then stitch the green circle to the centre of one white circle. Stitch the second white circle to the back using white thread and whip stitch.

For 32.5 (35, 40)cm, 13 (14, 16)in sizes:

Cut 4 circles of washable felt as follows:

2 x white measuring 5cm (2in) across.

1 x turquoise measuring 4cm (1½in) across.

1 x black measuring 2cm (¾in) across.

Stitch the black pupil to the centre of the turquoise circle then stitch the turquoise circle to the centre of the white circle. Stitch the second white circle to the back using white thread and whip stitch.

Crochet Eye

For 18 (19½)in, 45 (49)cm sizes:

* Using a 4mm (US G, 6) crochet hook and MC, make 2 ch. Work 7 dc into the first of the 2 ch. The eye is worked in a spiral. Use a length of yarn to mark the start of the round.

Round 1: 2dc into every st. (14 sts)

Round 2: [1dc, 2dc into next st] to the end. (21 sts)

Round 3: [2dc, 2dc into next st] to the end. (28 sts)

Change to CC1.

Round 4: [3dc, 2dc into next st] to the end. (35 sts)

Change to CC2.

Round 5: [4dc, 2dc into next st] to the end.

(42 sts). Sl st into next st, cut yarn and pull through loop on hook. Weave yarns ends into work and trim. Cut a black felt pupil measuring 2cm (¾in) across. Stitch to the centre of the eye with black thread.

For 32.5 (35, 40)cm, 13 (14, 16)in sizes: Follow all instructions from * to the end of Round 4, using MC for Rounds 1-3 and CC2 for Round 4. After Round 4, sl st into next st, cut yarn and pull through loop on hook. Weave yarns ends into work and trim. Add a black felt pupil as above.

Mouth and Tooth

Using 3.25mm (US 3) DPNS and CC3, cast on 2 sts. Knit an i-cord for approximately 10cm (4in). Cut yarn and cast off the 2 sts. For the tooth, cut 2 small triangles of white felt. Using white thread, whip stitch around all sides.

Braids

Cut 3 x 100cm (40in) lengths of CC1 and 6 x 100cm (40in) lengths of MC. Using a crochet hook, pull 3 lengths of MC halfway through a stitch at the base of earflap 1. Pull 3 lengths of CC1 halfway through the next st along then pull the remaining 3 lengths of MC halfway through the next st along. You now have 6 pieces of yarn in each of the 3 sections. Secure the hat between your knees and braid or plait the 3 sections of yarn together. Make a knot at the end to secure the braids and trim ends straight.

Making Up

Pin one spike in CC1 to the centre top of the hat. Pin the 2 spikes in MC on either side of the centre spike, leaving 2cm (¾in) gap. **For 45 (49)cm, 18 (19½)in sizes:** pin the remaining spikes in place leaving a 2cm (¾in) gap. Stitch in place with matching yarn. Pin the eye to centre-front of the hat and stitch in place. Slip stitch the mouth in place then stitch the tooth to one side of the mouth.

Round 9: [K2, K2tog] to the end. 18 (21, 24, 27, 30) sts

Round 11: [K1, K2tog] to the end. 12 (14, 16, 18, 20) sts

Round 13: [K2tog] to the end. 6 (7, 8, 9, 10) sts Cut yarn leaving a long tail end. Thread tail end on to a tapestry needle and gather the remaining sts. Pull tight and secure with a few stitches. Weave all loose ends into of hat and trim.

Spikes

For 32.5 (35, 40)cm, 13 (14, 16)in sizes: use 3.75mm (US 5) needles. **For 45 (49)cm, 18 (19½)in sizes:** use 4mm (US 6) needles. Using MC and correct needles, cast on 18 sts.

Row 1 (RS): K.

Row 2 (WS): P.

Row 3: [K1, SSK, K3, K2tog, K1] twice. (14 sts)

Rows 4–6: Starting with a P row, work 3 rows in st st.

Row 7: [K1, SSK, K1, K2tog, K1] twice. (10 sts)

Row 8–10: Starting with a P row, work 3

Big One-Eye!

What's better than one mini monster eye? A big monster eye to join the fun!

Finished Circumference

55cm or 22in
To fit an adult

Note: Instructions are provided for both a crochet eye and a felt eye

Construction

Knitted in the round

Techniques

Cast on, cast off, knit, purl, increase (M1, KFB), decrease (K2tog, SSK), making a braid, optional crochet (dc in the round)

Materials

Yarn

Rowan All Seasons Cotton:
- 2 x 50g (1¾oz) balls Jacuzzi (239) – MC
- 1 x 50g (1¾oz) ball Lime (241) – CC1
- Scraps of Organic (178) or worsted weight cream yarn – CC2
- Scraps of Black DK yarn – CC3

Needles

- 4.5mm (US 7) needles
- 3.75 or 4mm (US 5 or 6) needles
- 3.25mm (US 3) DPNS
- 4.5mm (US 7) circular needles, 40cm (16in)
- 5mm (US 8) circular needles, 40cm (16in)
- Set of 4 or 5 5mm (US 8) DPNS
- 4mm (US G,6) crochet hook

Notions

- Scraps of washable felt in turquoise, lime green, black and white for the felt eye
- 4mm (US G, 6) crochet hook and scraps of black washable felt for the crochet eye
- Sewing thread in black, white, green and turquoise, needle
- Scraps of white washable felt for teeth
- Stitch marker

Tension

16 sts and 23 rows to 10cm (4in) using 5mm (US 8) needles or correct size needed to achieve this tension.

Instructions

Earflaps (make 2)

Using 4.5mm (US 7) needles and MC, cast on 4 sts.
Row 1 (RS): K
Row 2 (WS): K1, P to last st, K1.
Row 3: K1, [KFB] twice, K1. (6 sts)
Row 4: K1, P to last st, K1.
Row 5: K1, KFB, K to last 2 sts, KFB, K1. (8 sts)
Row 6: Repeat row 4.
Repeat Rows 5 and 6 until 18 sts are on the needle.
Next Row: K.
Next Row: K1, P to last st, K1.
Repeat last 2 rows once more. Cut yarn and leave sts on needle. Repeat all instructions to make second ear flap.

Hat Border

Using MC and 4.5mm (US 7) circular needles, cast on 87 sts. Join in the round ready to start knitting and place marker for beginning of round.
Join the earflaps on Round 1 below, using the three-needle knitting technique. When instructed, arrange needles parallel to each other with earflap stitches in front of the cast-on stitches with RS of earflap facing you and knit both sets of corresponding stitches together. The centre-front stitches create a moss stitch border.
Round 1: K12 sts, join first earflap over the next 18 sts, [P1, K1] 13 times, P1, join second earflap over the next 18 sts, K12 sts. (87 sts)
Round 2: K31 sts, [P1, K1] 13 times. K29, KFB. (88 sts)

Main Hat

Change to 5mm (US 8) using circular needles, join CC1 (do not cut MC) and work 2 rounds of st st in CC1.
Cut CC1; continue working st st in MC until hat measures 17.5cm (7in) from border cast on.

Decreasing

Transfer stitches evenly between 3 or 4 5mm (US 8) DPNS before starting the de-

crease rounds. Use the spare DPN to start knitting.

Round 1: (K6, K2tog) to the end. (77 sts)
Round 2 and every alternate round: K.
Round 3: (K5, K2tog) to the end. (66 sts)
Round 5: (K4, K2tog) to the end. (55 sts)
Round 7: (K3, K2tog) to the end. (44 sts)
Round 9: (K2, K2tog) to the end. (33 sts)
Round 11: (K1, K2tog) to the end. (22 sts)
Round 13: (K2tog) to the end. (11 sts)
Cut yarn leaving a long tail end. Thread on to a darning needle and gather the remaining sts. Pull tight and secure with a few sts. Weave all loose yarn ends into WS of hat; trim.

Spikes

Using MC and 4mm (US 6) needles, cast on 18 sts.
Row 1 (RS): K.
Row 2 (WS): P.
Row 3: [K1, SSK, K3, K2tog, K1] twice. (14 sts).
Rows 4-6: Starting with a P row, work 3 rows in st st.
Row 7: [K1, SSK, K1, K2tog, K1] twice. (10 sts)
Row 8-10: Starting with a P row, work 3 rows in st st.
Row 11: [K1, K3tog, K1] twice. (6 sts)
Row 12: [P3tog] twice. (2 sts). Cut yarn leaving a long tail. Thread tail end on to a darning needle and gather the remaining sts. Pull tight and secure with a few sts. Fold spike in half and stitch all seams using mattress stitch with WS together. Make 1 more spike in MC and 3 in CC1.

Felt Eye

Cut 5 circles of washable felt as follows:
2 x white measuring 7.5cm (3in) across.
1 x green measuring 5cm (2in) across.
1 x turquoise measuring 4cm (1½in) across.
1 x black measuring 2cm (¾in) across.
Stitch the pupil to the centre of the turquoise circle. Stitch the turquoise circle to the centre of the green circle then stitch the green circle to the centre of one white circle. Stitch the second white circle to the back using white thread and whip stitch.

Crochet Eye

Using a 4mm (US G, 6) crochet hook and MC, make 2 ch. Work 7 dc into the first of the 2 ch. The eye is worked in a spiral. Use a length of yarn to mark the start of the round.
Round 1: 2dc into every st. (14 sts)
Round 2: [1dc, 2dc into next st] to the end. (21 sts)
Round 3: [2dc, 2dc into next st] to the end. (28 sts)
Change to CC1.
Round 4: [3dc, 2dc into next st] to the end, (35 sts)
Change to CC2.
Round 5: [4dc, 2dc into next st] to the end, sl st into next st, cut yarn and pull through loop on hook (42 sts). Sl st into next st, cut yarn and pull through loop on hook. Weave yarn ends into work and trim. Cut a black pupil from washable felt measuring 2cm

(¾in) across. Stitch to the centre of the eye with black thread.

Mouth and Tooth

Using 3.25mm (US 3) DPNS and CC3, cast on 2 sts. Knit an i-cord for approximately 10cm (4in). Cut yarn and cast off the 2 sts. For the tooth, cut 2 small triangles of white washable felt. Using white thread, whip stitch around all sides.

Making Up

Pin one spike in CC1 to the centre top of the hat. Pin the 2 spikes in MC on either side of the centre spike, leaving 2cm (¾in) gap. Pin the remaining spikes in place leaving a 2cm (¾in) gap. Stitch in place with matching yarn. Pin the eye to centre-front of the hat and stitch in place. Slip stitch the mouth in place then stitch the tooth to one side of the mouth.

Little Devil

Turn your little angel into a devil with this cute and easy hat. It is great for Halloween, costume parties or just for fun.

Finished Circumference
32.5 (35, 40, 45, 49)cm, 13 (14, 16, 18, 19.5)in
To fit up to 6mths (6–12 mths, 12–18 mths, toddler to child, child to pre-teen)

Materials
Yarn
- King Cole Merino Blend Double Knitting in the following shades:
- 1 (1, 1, 2, 2) x 50g (1¾oz) ball Scarlet (9) – MC
- 1 x 50g (1¾oz) ball Black (46) – CC

Needles
- 3.25mm (US 3) circular needles, 40cm (16in)
- 4mm (US 6) circular needles, 40cm (16in)
- 3.75mm (US 5) DPNS
- 3.75mm (US 5) straight needles

Notions
- Stitch marker
- Pins

Construction
Knitted in the round

Techniques
Cast on, cast off, knit, purl, increase (M1L, M1R), decrease (K2tog, Sl2, K1, PSSO, SSK), knitting in the round, knitting with DPNS, making an i-cord

Tension
22 sts and 30 rows to 10cm (4in) using 4mm (US 6) needles or correct size needed to achieve this tension

Instructions

Border

Using 3.25mm (US 3) circular needles and
CC, cast on 84 (90, 102, 114, 126) sts. Join for
working in the round and place marker to
indicate beginning of round. Work in garter
st for 6 rounds (when working in the round
this is one row knit, one row purl, repeated).
Change to MC and 4mm (US 6) circular
needles and commence chevron pattern:

Round 1: [K1, M1L, K12 (13, 15, 17, 19) Sl2, K1,
P2SSO, K12 (13, 15, 17, 19) M1R] 3 times.

Round 2: K.

Repeat Rounds 1 and 2 until work measures
6 (8.5, 10, 13, 13)cm, 2½ (3½, 4, 5, 5)in
from beginning (ending after a Round 2),
measuring length at centre-front peak.

Decreasing

Round 1: K13 (14, 16, 18, 20) Sl2, K1, P2SSO,
K25 (27, 31, 35, 39) Sl2, K1, P2SSO, K25 (27, 31,
35, 39) Sl2, K1, P2SSO, K12 (13, 15, 17, 19).
78 (84, 96, 108, 120) sts

Round 2 and every alternate round: K.

Round 3: K12 (13, 15, 17, 19) Sl2, K1, P2SSO,
K23 (25, 29, 33, 37) Sl2, K1, P2SSO, K23 (25,
29, 33, 37) Sl2, K1, P2SSO, K11 (12, 14, 16, 18).
72 (78, 90, 102, 114) sts

Round 5: K11 (12, 14, 16, 18) Sl2, K1, P2SSO,
K21 (23, 27, 31, 35) Sl2, K1, P2SSO, K21 (23, 27,
31, 35) Sl2, K1, P2SSO, K10 (11, 13, 15, 17).
66 (72, 84, 96, 108) sts

Round 7: K10 (11, 13, 15, 17) Sl2, K1, P2SSO,
K19 (21, 25, 29, 33) Sl2, K1, P2SSO, K19 (21, 25,
29, 33) Sl2, K1, P2SSO, K9 (10, 12, 14, 16).
60 (66, 78, 90, 102) sts

Round 9: K9 (10, 12, 14, 16) Sl2, K1, P2SSO,
K17 (19, 23, 27, 31) Sl2, K1, P2SSO, K17 (19, 23,
27, 31) Sl2, K1, P2SSO, K8 (9, 11, 13, 15). 54 (60,
72, 84, 96) sts

After Round 10, change to 4mm (US 6)
DPNS and start to decrease on every
round as follows:

Round 11: K8 (9, 11, 13, 15) Sl2, K1, P2SSO, K15
(17, 21, 25, 29) Sl2, K1, P2SSO, K15 (17, 21, 25,
29) Sl2, K1, P2SSO, K7 (8, 10, 12, 14). 48 (54,
66, 78, 90) sts

Round 12: K7 (8, 10, 12, 14) Sl2, K1, P2SSO,
K13 (15, 19, 23, 27) Sl2, K1, P2SSO, K13 (15, 19,
23, 27) Sl2, K1, P2SSO, K6 (7, 9, 11, 13). 42 (48,
60, 72, 84) sts

Round 13: K6 (7, 9, 11, 13) Sl2, K1, P2SSO, K11

(13, 17, 21, 25) Sl2, K1, P2SSO, K11 (13, 17, 21, 25) Sl2, K1, P2SSO, K5 (6, 8, 10, 12). 36 (42, 54, 66, 78) sts

Round 14: K5 (6, 8, 10, 12) Sl2, K1, P2SSO, K9 (11, 15, 19, 23) Sl2, K1, P2SSO, K9 (11, 15, 19, 23) Sl2, K1, P2SSO, K4 (5, 7, 9, 11). 30 (36, 48, 60, 72) sts

Round 15: K4 (5, 7, 9, 11) Sl2, K1, P2SSO, K7 (9, 13, 17, 21) Sl2, K1, P2SSO, K7 (9, 13, 17, 21) Sl2, K1, P2SSO, K3 (4, 6, 8, 10). 24 (30, 42, 54, 66) sts

Round 16: K3 (4, 6, 8, 10) Sl2, K1, P2SSO, K5 (7, 11, 15, 19) Sl2, K1, P2SSO, K5 (7, 11, 15, 19) Sl2, K1, P2SSO, K2 (3, 5, 7, 9). 18 (24, 36, 48, 60) sts

Round 17: K2 (3, 5, 7, 9) Sl2, K1, P2SSO, K3 (5, 9, 13, 17) Sl2, K1, P2SSO, K3 (5, 9, 13, 17) Sl2, K1, P2SSO, K1 (2, 4, 6, 8). 12 (18, 30, 42, 54) sts

For 32.5cm, 13in size: cut yarn, leaving a long tail. Thread on to a tapestry needle, gather remaining 12 sts. Pull tight, secure with stitches. Weave loose ends into WS of hat; trim.

For all other sizes: continue.

Round 18: K2 (4, 6, 8) Sl2, K1, P2SSO, K3 (7, 11, 15) Sl2, K1, P2SSO, K3 (7, 11, 15) Sl2, K1, P2SSO, K1 (3, 5, 7). 12 (24, 36, 48) sts

For 35cm, 14in size: Cut yarn, leaving a long tail. Thread on to a tapestry needle, gather remaining 12 sts. Pull tight, secure with stitches. Weave loose ends into WS of hat; trim.

For all other sizes: continue.

Round 19: K3 (5, 7) Sl2, K1, P2SSO, K5 (9, 13) Sl2, K1, P2SSO, K5 (9, 13) Sl2, K1, P2SSO, K2 (4, 6). 18 (30, 42) sts

Round 20: K2 (4, 6) Sl2, K1, P2SSO, K3 (7, 11) Sl2, K1, P2SSO, K3 (7, 11) Sl2, K1, P2SSO, K1 (3, 5). 12 (24, 36) sts. **For 40cm, 16in size:** cut yarn leaving a long tail end. Thread tail end on to a darning needle and gather the remaining 12 sts. Pull tight and secure with a few stitches. Weave all loose ends into WS of hat and trim.

For all other sizes: continue.

Round 21: K3 (5) Sl2, K1, P2SSO, K5 (9) Sl2, K1, P2SSO, K5 (9) Sl2, K1, P2SSO, K2 (4). 18 (30) sts

Round 22: K2 (4), Sl2, K1, P2SSO, K3 (7) Sl2, K1, P2SSO, K3 (7) Sl2, K1, P2SSO, K1 (3). 12 (24) sts

For 45cm (18in) size: cut yarn leaving a long tail end. Thread tail end on to a darning needle and gather the remaining 16 sts. Pull tight and secure with a few stitches. Weave loose ends WS of hat; trim.

For 49cm, 19½in size: continue.

Round 23: K3, Sl2, K1, P2SSO, K5, Sl2, K1, P2SSO, K5, Sl2, K1, P2SSO, K2. (18 sts)

Round 24: K2, Sl2, K1, P2SSO, K3, Sl2, K1, P2SSO, K3, Sl2, K1, P2SSO, K1. (12 sts)

Cut yarn leaving a long tail end. Thread tail end on to a darning needle and gather the remaining 12 sts. Pull tight and secure with a few stitches. Weave all loose ends into WS of hat and trim.

Horns (make 2)

Using CC1 and 3.75mm (US 5) straight needles, cast on 18 sts.

Row 1: K.

Row 2 and every alternate row: P.

Row 3: K6, SSK, K2, K2tog, K6. (16 sts)

Row 5: K5, SSK, K2, K2tog, K5. (14 sts)

Row 7: K4, SSK, K2, K2tog, K4. (12 sts)

Row 9: K3, SSK, K2, K2tog, K3. (10 sts)

Row 11: K2, SSK, K2, K2tog, K2. (8 sts)

Row 13: K1, SSK, K2, K2tog, K1. (6 sts)

Row 15: SSK, K2, K2tog. (4 sts)

After Row 15, cut yarn, thread on to a tapestry needle and gather the remaining 4 sts. Use the rest of the yarn tail to sew the seam of the horn together.

Pin the horns, facing forward, to the top of the hat, either side of the centre line, then stitch in place with CC.

Side Ties (Optional)

Using CC and two 3.75mm (US 5) DPNS, pick up and K4 sts from ear points. Knit an i-cord for 20cm (8in) or longer. Work the triangular end in rows as follows:

Using a two-needle method, cast on 4 sts. (8 sts)

Row 1: K to the end.

Row 2: Cast on 4 sts, K to the end. (12 sts)

Row 3: K to last 3 sts, K2tog, K1. (11 sts)

Row 4: As Row 3. (10 sts)

Rows 5–6: K.

Rows 7–14: Repeat Rows 3–6 three times. (4 sts)

Row 15: [K2tog] twice. (2 sts)

Row 16: K.

Row 17: K2tog. (1 st)

Cut yarn, leaving a long tail. Thread onto a tapestry needle and cast off. Pull though last st. Weave end into the triangle; trim.

Witch

Bewitch your friends with this cute and easy hat designed by Tracey Todhunter. It is perfect for Halloween or whenever you want to cast a spell.

Finished Circumference
32.5 (35, 40, 45, 49)cm or 14 (16, 18, 19½)in
To fit 6–12 mths (12–18 mths, toddler to child, child to pre-teen)

Note: There is no hat size for newborns.

Construction
Knitted in the round using magic loop technique

Techniques
Cast on, cast off, knit, purl, increase (M1, KFB), knitting on circular needles using magic loop technique, i-cord, increasing (KFB), decreasing (K2tog).

Materials
Yarn
King Cole Merino Blend Aran:
• 1 (1, 2, 2) x 50g (1¾oz) ball Black (775) – MC
• 1 x 50g (1¾oz) ball Lawn Green (768) – CC

Needles
• 4.5mm (US 7) circular needle, 80cm (30in)
• 5mm (US 8) circular needle, 80cm (30in)

Notions
• Locking stitch marker
• Star-shaped buttons, needle and matching thread
• Scraps of black and white washable felt for eyes and matching sewing threads and needle
• Small piece of hollow fibre filling for spider
• Small piece of touch and close, popper or snap fastener to attach spider

Tension
18 sts and 24 rows to 10cm (4in) on 5mm (US 8) needles or correct size needed to achieve this tension

Special Instructions
This hat is worked in the round from the top down using magic loop technique. This allows for the hat to be tailored exactly to the recipient's head and for the frilled brim to be knitted on without having to pick up and knit.

As the hat has no ribbing it is designed with negative ease as stocking stitch can be very stretchy.

The hat begins with 4.5mm (US 7) needle to give a firm point to the top of the hat.

When changing colours, green yarn should be twisted round black and 'carried' up around instead of being cut off and rejoined.

Instructions

Using 4.5mm (US 7) needles, cast on 8 sts.
Work an i-cord for 0.5 (0.5, 1, 1)cm, ¼ (¼, ½, ½)in.

Arrange sts so there are 4 on each side of needle and continue working in the round using magic loop method. Use locking stitch marker to indicate first stitch of needle 1 and remove and replace on each round.

Round 1: [K1, KFB] to end. (12 sts)
Round 2: K.
Round 3: [K2, KFB] to end. (16 sts)
Round 4: K.
Round 5: [K3, KFB] to end. (20 sts)
Round 6: Change to CC, K to end.
Round 7: With MC, K to end.
Round 8: [K4, KFB] to end. (24 sts)
Round 9: K.
Round 10: [K5, KFB] to end. (28 sts)
Rounds 11–12: As Rounds 6–7.
Round 13: [K6, KFB] to end. (32 sts)
Round 14: K.
Round 15: [K7, KFB] to end. (36 sts)
Rounds 16–17: Repeat Rounds 6–7.
Round 18: [K8, KFB] to end. (40 sts)
Round 19: K.
Round 20: [K9, KFB] to end. (44 sts)
Rounds 21–22: Rep Rounds 6–7.
Round 23: [K10, KFB] to end. (48 sts)
Round 24: K.
Round 25: [K11, KFB] to end. (52 sts)
Rounds 26–27: Repeat Rounds 6–7.
Round 28: [K12, KFB] to end. (56 sts)
Round 29: K.
Round 30: [K13, KFB] to end. (60 sts)
For 35cm, 14in size: jump to 'Shape Brim'.
For all other sizes: continue.
Rounds 31–32: Repeat Rounds 6–7.
Round 33: [K14, KFB] to end. (64 sts)
For 40cm, 16in size jump to 'Shape Brim'.
For all other sizes: continue.
Round 34: K.
Round 35: [K15, KFB]. (68 sts)

Rounds 36–37: Rep Rounds 6–7.
Round 38: [K16, KFB] to end. (72 sts)
For 45cm, 18in size: skip to 'Shape Brim'.
For 49cm, 19½in size: continue.
Round 39: K.
Round 40: [K17, KFB] to end. (76 sts)

Shape Brim (all sizes)

Work in st st until hat measures 15 (17.5, 20, 20)cm, 6 (7, 8, 8)in from round 1 then continue as follows:
Round 1: With CC, K to end.
Round 2: Change to US 7 (4.5mm) needles and MC and K to end.
Rounds 3–5: K.
Round 6: P.
Round 7: [KFB] to end. 120 (128, 144, 152) sts
Rounds 8–10: K.
Round 11: [KFB] to end. 240 (256, 288, 304) sts
Rounds 12–14: K.
Cast off.

Finishing

Weave in all ends and block lightly. Sew buttons on to hat, using the photograph as a guide.

Spider Instructions

Spider is worked flat and seamed.

Legs

* Using 4.5mm (US 7) needles and MC cast on 3 stitches. Knit an i-cord until work measures 10cm (4in). Cast off.**
Repeat from * to ** three times.
Make another i-cord 25cm (10in) long.

Body

Using 4.5mm (US 7) needles and MC, cast on 5 sts.
Row 1 (RS): K1, KFB, K to last 2 sts, KFB, K1. (7 sts).
Row 2 (WS): P.
Row 3: As row 1. (9 sts)
Rows 4–8: Starting with a P row, work 5 rows in st st.
Row 9: K1, K2tog, K to last 3 sts, K2tog, K1.

(7 sts)
Row 10: P.
Row 11: Repeat Row 9. (5 sts)
Row 12: P.
Repeat rows 1–12 once more. Cast off.

Making Up

Join the four pieces of i-cord in the centre to make 8 legs. Fold body in half and place legs in centre, add a small piece of stuffing and sew around body using mattress stitch. Cut 4 small 1cm (¼in) circles of white felt (2 for each eye—one front, one back). Cut smaller circles of black and stitch each black circle to the front of each white eye then stitch the front of each white eye to the back using whip stitch and white thread. Stitch each eye to the front of the spider. Attach long piece of i-cord to centre top of body and stitch one side of snap or popper to opposite end. Stitch the other side of the snap or popper to the hat, using the photograph as a guide.

Ogre

It is the witching hour
and the ogres are out!
This fun hat is perfect
for Halloween, or all year
round for monster fans.

Finished Circumference

32.5 (35, 40, 45, 49)cm or 13 (14, 16, 18, 19½)in
To fit up to 6 mths (6–12 mths, 12–18 mths,
toddler to child, child to pre-teen)

Construction

Knitted in the round

Techniques

Cast on, cast off, knit, purl, increase (M1),
decrease (K2tog), knitting on circular
needles, knitting with DPNS

Materials

Yarn

King Cole Merino Blend DK:
- 1 (2, 2, 2, 2) x 50g (1¾oz) ball Lime Green
  (6315) – MC

Needles

- 4mm (US 6) circular needle, 40cm (16in)
- 3.25mm (US 3) DPNS
- Set of 4 or 5 4mm (US 6) DPNS needles
- Set of 4 or 5 3.25mm (US 6) DPNS

Notions

- Stitch marker

Tension

22 sts and 30 rows to 4 in (10cm) using US 6
(4mm) needles or correct size needed to
achieve this tension

Pull tight and secure with a few stitches. Weave all loose ends into WS of work and trim.

Ear Trumpets (make 2)

Using 3.25mm (US 3) DPNS, cast on 14 sts and divide over 3 needles. Join in the round ready to start knitting with 4th DPN and place marker. Work in st st until ear trumpet measures 4cm (1½in).
Next round: K1, [M1, K2] to last st, M1, K1. (21 sts)
Next round: K.
Next round: K2, [M1, K3] to last st, M1, K1. (28 sts)
Work 5 more rounds in st st. Cast off knitwise. Cut yarn and pull through last st. Weave yarn end into work; trim. Position ear trumpets to the sides of the hat, stitch in place using mattress stitch. Roll down the cast-off edge of each ear trumpet.

Instructions

Main Hat

Using 4mm (US 6) circular needles, cast on 72 (78, 88, 98, 108) sts. Join in the round, and place marker to indicate beginning of round. Work in st st until hat measures 11.5 (14, 16.5, 19, 19)cm, 4½ (5½, 6½, 7½, 7½)in.

Decreasing

For 35 (45, 49)cm, 14 (18, 19½)in sizes: [K11 (47, 25) K2tog] to end. 72 (96, 104) sts
For all sizes: Transfer sts evenly between 3 or 4 DPNS; use the spare DPN to start knitting.
Round 1: [K6, K2tog] to end. 63 (63, 77, 84, 91) sts
Round 2 and every alternate round: K.
Round 3: [K5, K2tog] to end. 54 (54, 66, 72, 78) sts
Round 5: [K4, K2tog] to end. 45 (45, 55, 60, 65) sts
Round 7: [K3, K2tog] to end. 36 (36, 44, 48, 52) sts
Round 9: [K2, K2tog] to end. 27 (27, 33, 36, 39) sts
Round 11: [K1, K2tog] to end. 18 (18, 22, 24, 26) sts
Round 13: [K2tog] to end. 9 (9, 11, 12, 13) sts
Cut yarn leaving a long tail. Thread onto a tapestry needle and gather remaining sts.

Finished Circumference

32.5 (35, 40, 45, 49)cm or 13 (14, 16, 18, 19½)in
To fit up to 6 mths (6–12mths, 12–18 mths,
toddler to child, child to pre-teen)

Construction

Knitted in the round

Techniques

Cast on, cast off, knit, purl, increase (M1,
KFB), decrease (K2tog), knitting in the
round, knitting with DPNS

Materials

Yarn

• Rowan All Seasons Cotton:
• 1 (2, 2, 2, 2) x 50g (1¾oz) ball Lime (241) – CC

Needles

• 5mm (US 8) circular needles, 40cm (16in)
• 4 or 5 5mm (US 8) DPNS

Notions

• White washable felt for eyes
• Scraps of black washable felt for eyes
• Black and white sewing thread and needle
• Stitch marker

Tension

16 sts and 23 rows to 10cm (4in) using 5mm
(US 8) needles or correct size needed to
achieve this tension

Aliens Have Landed!

They are here and looking for a new home with all three of their eyes! Will they find a place with you?

Instructions

Main Hat

Using 5mm (US 8) circular needles, cast on 52 (56, 64, 72, 78) sts. Join in the round, place marker to indicate beginning of round. Work in st st until hat measures 11.25 (13.75, 16.25, 18.75, 18.75)cm, 4½ (5½, 6½, 7½, 7½)in. The cast-on edge of the hat will roll up to create a brim.

Decreasing

For 32.5 (49)cm, 13 (19½)in sizes: [K11, K2tog] to end. 48 (72) sts

For all sizes:
Transfer stitches evenly between 3 or 4 DPNS and use the spare DPN to start knitting.

Round 1: [K6, K2tog] to end. 42 (49, 56, 63, 63) sts

Round 2 and every alternate round: K.

Round 3: [K5, K2tog] to end. 36 (42, 48, 54, 54) sts

Round 5: [K4, K2tog] to end. 30 (35, 48, 45, 45) sts

Round 7: [K3, K2tog] to end. 24 (28, 32, 36, 36) sts

Round 9: [K2, K2tog] to end. 18 (21, 24, 27, 27) sts

Round 11: [K1, K2tog] to end. 12 (14, 16, 18, 18) sts

Round 13: [K1 (1, 0, 0, 0) K2tog] to last 0 (2, 0, 0, 0) sts. For 35cm (14in) size only: K2tog. 8 (9, 8, 9, 9) sts. Do not cut yarn, continue with antenna on DPNS.

Antenna

Work in st st until antenna measures 4 (4, 5, 5, 5)cm, 1½ (1½, 2, 2, 2)in.

Next round: KFB into every st. 16 (18, 16, 18, 18) sts. Work 7 more rounds in st st. Cast off knitwise. Cut yarn, pull through last st. Weave end into work and trim. Roll down bound off edge of the antenna down to the increase round.

Eyes

Cut 6 circles from white washable felt that measure approximately 3cm (1¼in) across (2 for each eye). Cut 3 smaller circles from black washable felt (1 pupil per eye). Stitch each black pupil to the centre of one white eye front, using whip stitch and black thread. Stitch the front of the eye to the back using whip stitch and white thread. Slip stitch the 3 eyes across the front of the main hat, with the centre eye slightly higher than the other 2 eyes. Locate the centre eye approximately 4cm (1½in) below the antenna, then the other two eyes slightly lower so that the eyes create an arc shape.

Techniques and equipment

Whether you are fairly new to knitting or an old hand, this section will help you brush up on a problem area or a tricky technique. You will also learn how to make pompoms, fringes and other finishing touches that will bring your whimsical hats to life.

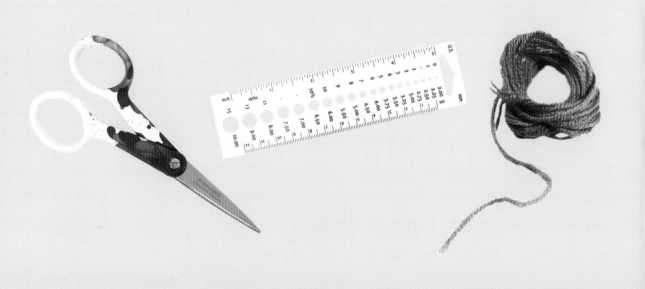

Equipment

All you really need to get started is a pair of knitting needles and some yarn, but depending on your skill level and the complexity of the project, you may need some additional equipment.

Knitting needles – straight

As the popularity of knitting has grown, so too has the range of needles. The most common types are made from either plastic, metal, bamboo or birch wood. They come in different sizes that work with different thicknesses of yarn.

The sizes quoted in the pattern instructions are a useful guide, but you might need to alter the size to achieve the correct fabric tension. If your tension is too loose, the project will be too big; if it is too tight, the result will be too small and will also use more yarn.

Knitting needles – double-pointed

Double-pointed needles come in sets of four or five and are generally used for creating smaller projects in the round, but they can also be used to work single-row stripes and to create i-cords.

Needle gauge

A needle gauge is very useful for checking or converting needle sizes, especially as the numbers printed on the needles can wear off with age.

Stitch holder

Stitch holders are used to hold stitches that you are not working with, rather than keeping them on your needles. If you are caught without a stitch holder you can always use a contrasting colour of yarn – slip the yarn through the stitches and knot the ends together.

Safety pins

A coiless safety pin can be used as a stitch holder if only a few stitches need to be held, or as a stitch marker if you do not have any to hand. They also come in handy if you need to catch a dropped stitch.

Row counter

A row counter fits neatly on the end of a knitting needle. Turn the dial as you work each row.

Stitch marker

Coloured plastic or metal rings, stitch markers are useful for marking stitches or rows.

Pins

Glass-headed rustproof dressmaking pins are the best type to use. Pins with brightly coloured heads are easy to see against the fabric.

Tape measure/ruler

Choose a tape measure and a clear plastic ruler that show both inches and centimetres.

Scissors

Scissors are an essential part of the knitting kit, and it is best to have several pairs for different uses.

Tapestry needle

Use a blunt-ended tapestry needle with a large eye to weave in ends and stitch pieces together. You can also use a darning or wool needle.

Reading a Pattern

It is important to read through the entire pattern before starting to knit any project so that you understand all the abbreviations. Yarn amounts, needle sizes and any extra equipment and materials will also appear at the beginning of each pattern.

Abbreviations

The patterns in this book feature a number of standard abbreviations, which are explained below.

alt	alternate	M1L	make 1 left increase	sc	single crochet
beg	begin(s), beginning	M1R	make 1 right increase	SK2PO	slip next stitch, knit next 2 sts together, pass slipped stitch over the K2tog (decrease 2 sts)
CC	contrasting colour	MC	main colour		
ch	chain	P	purl		
cont	continue	P2tog	purl 2 stitches together (decrease 1 st)	Sl1k	slip one knitwise
dec(s)	decrease(s), decreasing			Sl1p	slip one purlwise
DPN(S)	double-pointed needle(s)	P2togtbl	purl 2 stitches together through back loop (decrease 1 st)	sl st	slip stitch
inc(s)	increase(s), increasing			ssk	slip, slip, knit (decrease 1 st)
K	knit	patt	pattern(s)	st(s)	stitch(es)
K2tog	knit 2 stitches together (decrease 1 st)	Pfb	purl into the front and back loop of same stitch (increase 1 st)	st st	stocking stitch
				tbl	through back loop
K2togtbl	knit 2 stitches together through the back loop (decrease 1 st)	prev	previous(ly)	tog	together
		PSSO	pass slip stitch over (decrease 1 st)	WS	wrong side
KFB	knit into the front and back loop of same stitch (increase 1 st)	rem	remain, remaining	WSF	wrong side facing
		rep	repeat(s)	YO	yarn over (increase 1 st)
		RH	right hand	YOH	yarn over hook (crochet)
LH	left hand	rnd(s)	round(s)	*	repeat from *
M1	make 1 stitch	RS	right side		

Swatches and Tension

Tension (also known as gauge) is critical in knitting. It refers to the size of your stitches, which in turn affects the size of your finished project.

Every knitting pattern should state the tension that you need to achieve in order to make your project to the correct size. If you do not knit to the tension stated, your finished project will not match the dimensions in the pattern. If you knit a looser stitch or tension, your finished project will turn out larger than the pattern dimensions. On the other hand, if you knit a tighter stitch or tension your finished product will turn out smaller than the pattern dimensions. This can be devastating, especially if you have spent months knitting a jumper only to find that it looks more like dress than a jumper, or that it is far too small to fit over your head.

The key to knitting the perfect project is to check that you knit to the same tension as the pattern before you start knitting your project, using the same yarn and needles as the project recommends.

Substituting Yarns

If you want to use a different yarn than recommended, you must match the tension to the one given in the pattern. You will find all the information you need about a yarn on the ball band (the paper that is wrapped around a ball or skein of yarn). Check the yarn weight, fibre content and yardage and make sure it matches the yarn recommended. Knit up a swatch with your chosen yarn, following the instructions below, to make sure you can achieve the correct tension required.

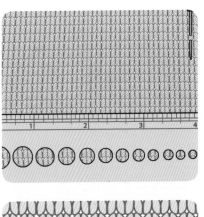

How to Knit a Tension Square (Swatch)

Your knitting pattern tells you how many stitches and rows should make a 10cm (4in) square over stocking stitch (or specified pattern), using a given size of needles and yarn type.

To make a tension square or swatch, cast on at least 10 more stitches than specified and knit at least 10 more rows than instructed. Cast off very loosely so as not to distort the top few rows of knitting. Next, place the square on a flat surface. Place a transparent ruler vertically across the square and measure 10cm (4in) in the centre of the square (ignore the edge sts). Mark the beginning and end of the 10cm (4in) length with pins. Do the same vertically and place pins as markers. Count how many stitches and how many rows there are between the pins. This is your tension.

If your stitch and row counts are the same as specified by the pattern you can go ahead and start knitting. If you have more stitches and rows, you are knitting too tightly and your project will end up too small. You will need to make another swatch with slightly larger needles and measure again.

If you have fewer stitches than specified, you are knitting too loosely and your project will be too large. You will need to make another swatch with slightly smaller needles and measure again.

Continue to swatch with different sized needles until you achieve the tension called for in the pattern.

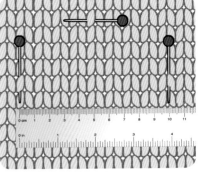

Knit and Purl

Most knitting is based on combinations of just two basic stitches – knit and purl. Once you have mastered these stitches, you can work many different stitch patterns. The knit stitch is the simplest of all stitches. Knitting every row forms the ridged fabric called garter stitch. When you work a row of knit stitches alternated with a row of purl stitches, this is referred to as stocking stitch.

Knit

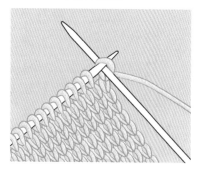

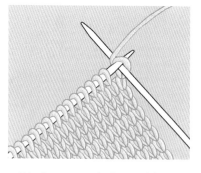

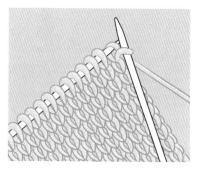

1. Hold the needle with the stitches to be knitted in your left hand with the yarn behind the work. Insert the right-hand needle into the first stitch on the needle from front to back.

2. Take the yarn over the first stitch from back to front, forming a loop.

3. Bring the needle and new loop to the front of the work through the stitch, and then slide the original stitch off the left-hand needle.

Purl

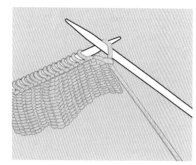

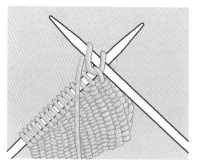

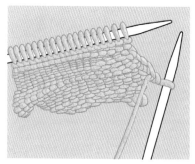

1. Hold the needle with the stitches to be purled in the left hand, with the yarn at the front of the work. Insert the right-hand needle through the front of the stitch, from right to left.

2. Take the yarn over and under the first stitch, forming a loop.

3. Take the needle and the new loop through the back and slide the original stitch off the left-hand needle.

Basic Stitch Variations

Once you have mastered your knit and purl stitches, countless fabric effects are, quite literally, at your fingertips. The art is to combine the two stitches together to create a world of variation in your knitting.

Garter Stitch

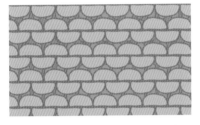

Garter stitch looks the same on both sides.

If you were to work rows of just knit, or rows of just purl stitches in succession, you would create a knitted fabric known as garter stitch. This is quite textural and sturdy and looks the same on both sides of the fabric.

Rib Stitch

Rib stitch can look the same on both sides.

A knit rib is simply a mix of knits and purls across a row. A rib can be any mix of knits and purls built up on top of each other in vertical lines or 'ribs'. A ribbed fabric is very stretchy and is therefore great in areas such as cuffs, where the fabric needs to grip more tightly to the body.

Moss Stitch (Seed Stitch)

Moss stitch also looks the same on both sides.

Moss stitch (also known as seed stitch) consists of single knit and purl stitches alternating both vertically and horizontally to create little bumps that look like scattered seeds. Moss stitch looks the same on both sides and lies flat, so is a good stitch for borders and edgings.
To create moss stitch with an even number of stitches:
Row 1: [K1, P1] to the end
Row 2: [P1, K1] to the end
Repeat Rows 1 and 2 until required length is reached.
To create moss stitch with an odd number of stitches:
Row 1: [K1, P1] to the last st, K1
Repeat Row 1 until required length is reached.

Stocking Stitch

Stocking stitch front or right side.

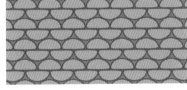

Reverse of stocking stitch.

Stocking stitch fabric is different on both sides and therefore has a right side, or front, and a wrong side, or back. The sides of the fabric are also respectively referred to as a knit side and a purl side. One side is smooth, and you will be able to see that the stitches create a zigzag effect. The other (reverse) side is bumpy and looks a little like garter stitch. To make a fabric using stocking stitch, work rows of knit stitches and rows of purl stitches alternately. If you have the smooth side of the fabric facing you as you begin the row, you will need to work a knit row in order to keep the pattern correct. If you have the more textural side facing you at the beginning of the row, you will need to work a purl row.

Casting On

Casting on is the first step in hand knitting and it provides the first row of loops on the needle. Different methods of casting on produce different types of edges. The diagrams below show the cable method, but if you are familiar with another method, you can use that instead.

Making a Slip Knot

A knitted fabric is made by working rows of stitches in various sequences. To create a fabric, you must first make a base row, known as a cast-on row. A slip knot is used as the first stitch for a cast-on row.

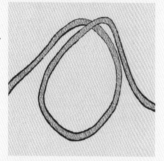

1. Holding the yarn in both hands, make a small loop. Take the piece that you are holding in the right hand underneath the loop.

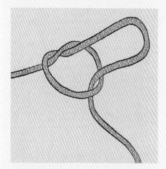

2. Pull this piece of yarn through the original loop to create a knot. Do not pull the short end of the yarn through the loop. Place the slip knot on to the knitting needle.

The Continental Cast On

The continental method can be worked by English or continental knitters. It is also called the long-tail or double cast-on method.

You need to leave a tail of approx 3–5 times as long as the desired cast-on edge. With this method, use your left hand to hold one needle and your right hand to hold the two strands of yarn – the short tail and the ball end.

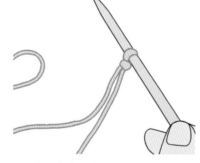

1. Make a slip knot, leaving the correct length of long tail and place on right needle.

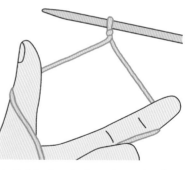

2. Grab both ends of yarn in your hand, with long tail on left, ball end to the right. Place thumb and index finger of left hand between yarn ends so that working yarn is around index finger and tail end is around thumb, making a diamond shape with the yarn.

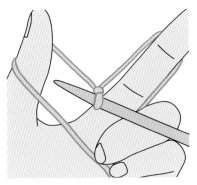

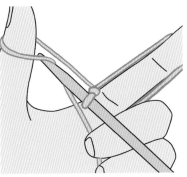

3. Pull needle downward to create a 'heart' type shape with the yarn.

4. Bring needle up through loop on thumb from bottom.

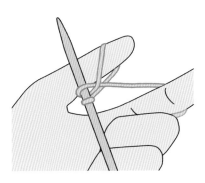

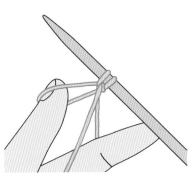

5. Draw loop from thumb up and grab a strand from around index finger with needle.

6. Draw loop from index finger back down through loop on thumb to create a stitch on the needle.

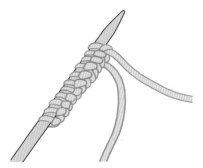

7. Drop loop off thumb and, placing thumb back through the centre of the two strands of yarn in the diamond configuration, tighten resulting stitch on needle. Rep steps 2–7 until you have cast on desired number of stitches.

The Cable Method

This cast-on method uses both knitting needles and creates a firm edge.

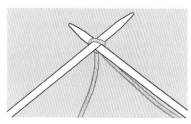

1. Place the slip knot onto the knitting needle and hold the needle in your left hand. Slide the right knitting needle through the loop created by the slip knot from front to back.

2. With your right hand, wrap the yarn around the right knitting needle counter-clockwise from back to front.

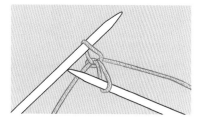

3. Slide the right needle through the loop on the left needle, catching the wrapped yarn and bringing it through the loop to create a new loop.

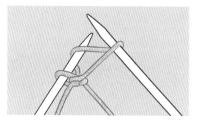

4. Pass the left needle over the top of the new loop, placing the tip of the needle through the loop on the right needle. Remove the right needle, thus transferring the stitch to the left needle.

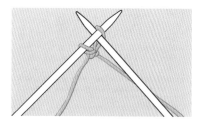

5. Make each subsequent stitch by placing the right needle between the last 2 stitches made on the left needle, and repeating Steps 2 through 4.

Casting Off

There is one simple and commonly used method of securing stitches once you have finished a piece of knitting known as cast-off. The most common – cable cast-off – is shown below. These diagrams show casting off along a knit row. However, you can cast off in pattern along any fabric, by working each stitch as set in pattern.

Cable Cast-off

Cable cast-off is worked using the two needles you have been working with all along.

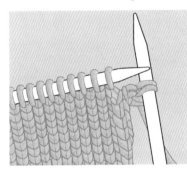

1. When you are ready to cast off, knit the first 2 stitches.

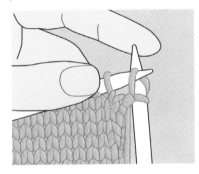

2. Slip the left-hand needle into the first stitch on the right-hand needle, and lift it over the second stitch and off the needle.

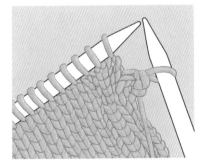

3. Knit the next stitch so that there are 2 stitches on the right-hand needle again.

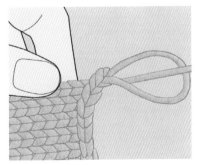

4. Repeat Steps 2 and 3 until all stitches have been worked and 1 stitch remains on the right-hand needle. Make the last stitch loop larger, break the yarn and draw through the loop to fasten off.

Shaping

Shaping techniques are used to create shapes in a piece of knitting.

Increasing (inc)

The two most common methods are Make 1 (M1), which creates an increase between two stitches, and increasing by knitting into the front and back of a stitch (KFB). Both are usually worked at least one stitch in from the edge to make sewing up and picking up stitches easier.

Make 1 (M1)

1. To make a left-slant increase (M1L), insert the right-hand needle from front to back beneath the horizontal bar of yarn between 2 stitches where you want the increase.

2. Slip the bar onto the left-hand needle.

3. Create the new stitch by knitting through the back of the loop. This twists the loop and avoids making a hole.

Note: To make a right slant increase (M1R – with left needle, lift strand between needles from back to front, knit lifted strand through the front.

Knit into Front and Back (KFB)

This means knitting into the front and then the back of the same stitch.

1. Work to where the extra stitch is needed. Knit into the front of the next stitch on the left knitting needle without slipping it off.

2. With the stitch still on the left needle and the yarn at the back, knit into the back of the same stitch and slip it from the needle.

Working Knit and Purl Stitches in the Same Row

Create textural relief patterns by working knit and purl stitches in the same row. It is important to change stitch correctly.

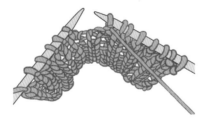 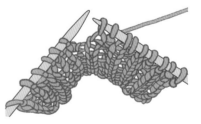

A. In changing from a purl to a knit stitch, the yarn will be held at the front of the work. Take the yarn to the back of the work between both knitting needles. Knit the next stitch.

B. In changing from a knit stitch to a purl stitch. Having completed a knit stitch, the yarn will be held at the reverse, back of the work. In order to work a subsequent purl stitch, bring the yarn through to the front of the work between both knitting needles, then purl the next stitch.

Decreasing (dec)

Decreasing techniques are used to make the fabric narrower by reducing the number of stitches. Various techniques are used, depending on whether the decrease needs to slant to the left or the right.

Slanting to the Right

Knit 2 stitches together (K2tog)

To decrease a stitch knitwise, insert the needle from left to right through the first 2 stitches on the left-hand needle and knit as you would normally, slipping both stitches off the needle at the same time.

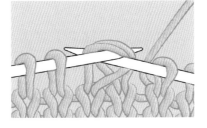 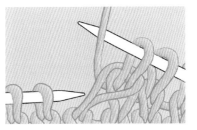

Purl 2 stitches together (P2tog)

To decrease a stitch purlwise, insert the needle from right to left through the first 2 stitches on the left-hand needle and purl as you would normally, slipping both stitches off the needle at the same time.

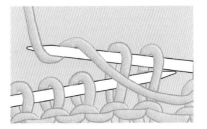 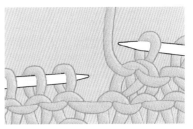

Slanting to the Left (ssk – slip, slip, knit)

  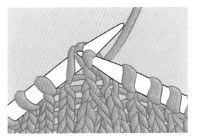

1. To decrease knitwise, slip 2 stitches knitwise one at a time from the left- to the right-hand needle.

2. Insert the tip of the left-hand needle from left to right through the front loop of both stitches.

3. Knit them together through the back loop.

Picking Up Stitches

Some knitting patterns will ask you to pick up stitches along either a horizontal or vertical edge. Stitches must be picked up evenly along the required edge using a knitting needle and yarn to create the stitches you will work into.

Horizontal Edge

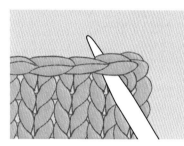

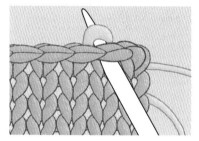

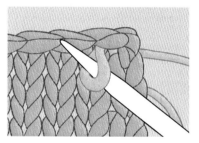

1. When picking up stitches along a bound-off or cast-on row, work into 1 full stitch above or below to give a neater finish. Holding the needle in your right hand, insert the tip into the centre of the first full stitch from the front to the back.

2. Wrap the yarn around the needle as if you were working a knit stitch.

3. Then pull the loop on the needle through to the front of the fabric to create a new stitch. Complete this until you have the required number of stitches.

Vertical Edge

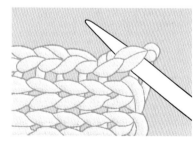

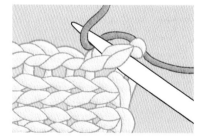

1. When picking up along an edge, work 1 full stitch in from the edge. Holding the needle in your right hand, insert the tip in between the first and second stitches from the front to the back.

2. Next wrap the yarn around the needle as if you were working a knit stitch, and then pull the loop on the needle through to the front of the fabric to create a new stitch. Complete this until you have the required amount of stitches.

Three-needle Knitting

Some of the earflaps on the hats in this book are joined after the cast-on round by knitting the earflap stitches at the same time as some of the cast-on stitches. This makes a really neat finish.

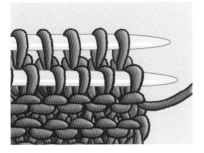

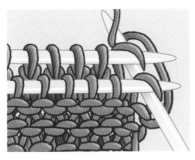

1. To knit two sets of stitches together, place the earflap stitches in front of the cast on stitches with right sides of both facing toward you. Hold both needles in your left hand and line up the corresponding stitches.

2. * Insert the empty right-hand needle into the first stitch on each of the two needles and knit the two stitches together with your working yarn (the yarn attached to the ball). Slip them off the needle as you would a knit stitch. You now have one stitch on the right needle. Continue from * until you have knitted the required number of stitches.

Making an i-cord

The i-cord or 'idiot cord' was created by Elizabeth Zimmerman, one of the most revered knitters in recent history, famous for her innovative techniques and instructional books. The i-cord is a simple technique that produces a narrow tube of knitting that looks a little like French knitting. I-cords can be used for a wide variety of purposes, from shoes laces, to bag handles, edgings and ties.

1. Using two double-pointed needles, cast on 2, 3, 4 or 5 stitches. The number of stitches cast on will depend on the thickness of your yarn and how thick you want your cord.
2. Knit the stitches.
3. Instead of turning your work, slide the stitches just worked to the opposite end of the needle, keeping the RS facing you. The yarn remains to the left of the stitches.

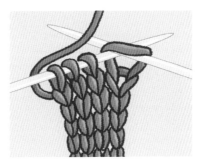

4. Pull the yarn tightly across the back of the stitches and knit another row.
5. Repeat Steps 3 and 4 until your cord reaches the length desired.
6. Cast off your stitches, cut yarn and pull it through the last stitch.

Circular Knitting

Circular knitting, or knitting in the round, is a term used to describe a method of knitting that creates a seamless fabric. The method can be worked on circular needles or on a set of four or five double-pointed needles (DPNS).

When working stocking stitch in the round, you never need to purl – just knit every row without turning, as you are are on the same side of the knitting. But to do garter stitch (usually knit every row), you will need to alternate between knit and purl rows.

There are many advantages to working with sets of four DPNS or a pair of circular needles, especially when using the Fair Isle technique or working neckbands or cuffs. The only technique that is tricky to work in the round is intarsia.

As with all knitting, work a swatch to judge the tension, as this can change when you are using a combination of knit and purl rows. However, do remember if you are working stocking stitch that the tension will be different from usual, as you will never have to do a purl row when working in the round – usually this purl row can differ greatly in tension. Therefore, you need to do your tension swatch in the round, too.

Circular Needles

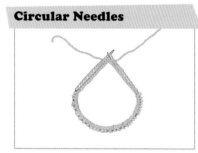

Make sure the circular needle you choose is long enough to hold the number of stitches in the pattern, but remember that if the length of needle is too long, the stitches will not stretch all the way around the cord to complete a round unless you use the magic loop. Cast on the stitches and spread them along the length of the circular needle, making sure that the row is not twisted. Mark the first stitch with a contrast thread or stitch marker to keep track of the beginning of the round. You can still create a flat piece of knitting with knit and purl rows using circular needles, which is great when knitting while on a journey, or if you are prone to losing needles. Simply turn the work at the end of every row and swap needles between hands.

Double-pointed Needles

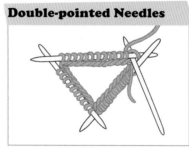

Double-pointed needles, or DPNS, are available in sets of four or five. Divide the stitches evenly between three or four of the needles and, once the cast-on row has been made, use the fourth or fifth needle to knit. Once all the stitches from one needle have been knitted onto the working needle, use the free needle to work the stitches along from the next needle. Keep the tension of the stitches constant when transferring from one needle to another; always draw the yarn up firmly when knitting the first stitch at the changeover point to avoid a ladder or loopy stitch. As with circular needles, ensure the cast-on row is not twisted before you start knitting and use a stitch marker to identify the first stitch.

Magic Loop

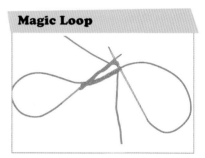

Cast on the stitches and divide them in half equally, placing half on one needle and the rest on the cord. Pull a length of cord through the gap between the sets of stitches. Make sure the row is not twisted. Join for working in the round by placing a marker for the first stitch of the round, then pull the right-hand needle slightly out of its stitches while leaving the other half of the stitches on the left-hand needle. Knit the stitches from the left-hand needle, using the right-hand needle, pulling tightly on the yarn for the first few stitches to ensure the round joins seamlessly. The right-hand needle will now have stitches on it, and the left-hand needle will not. Pull the cord so the stitches are on the left-hand needle. Pull out the right-hand needle, leaving its stitches on the cord so you can use it to knit off the left-hand needle. Continue for the required length.

How to Crochet

Read these instructions carefully, and remember that practice makes perfect. These can easily work whether you are left- or right-handed – use the hook in the hand that you write with. You can hold it like a pencil, or with the hook underneath your hand. Hold the hook however feels comfortable – there is no right or wrong way.

Making a Slip Knot

To begin almost all crochet, you will need to make a slip knot.

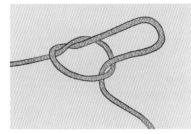

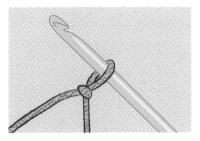

1. Make a loop with the yarn. Pull the tail end (the end not attached to the ball of yarn) through and tighten.

2. Place the slip knot on to the crochet hook and tug sharply to pull it tight.

Holding the Yarn

Once the slip knot is on the hook, hold your left hand out, palm up, or vice versa if you are left-handed. There are 2 ways of holding the yarn, shown below.

Place the tail of the yarn between your little and ring fingers and wrap it around the back of your hand. Point your index finger out and rest the yarn on your finger.

Another method of holding the working yarn is to wrap it twice around your index finger.

Making a Chain

The foundation chain is the first row, and resembles a braid or a series of V shapes.

1. Bring the hook under the yarn that rests on your index finger.

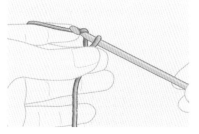

2. Wrap the yarn around the hook.

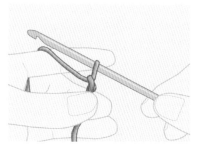

3. Pull the yarn through the loop on the hook.

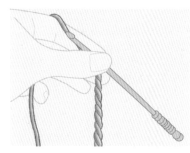

4. Repeat this until you have the desired amount of stitches.

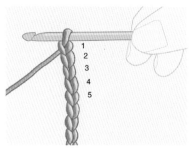

5. Count each chain stitch as you work them, but do not count the loop on your hook.

How to Slip Stitch (sl st)

This stitch is used for joining, or working along to the next point in the pattern while being invisible.

As you did for the foundation chain, insert the hook through the stitch and wrap the yarn over hook (YOH) by bringing your hook under the yarn resting on your finger and drawing it through the loop. You will now have 2 loops on your hook. Draw the first one through the second one, leaving you with 1 loop on the hook.

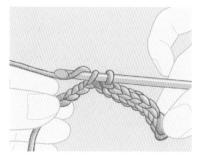

Double Crochet

This small stitch is tight and neat, perfect for working with shaped motifs. One side of your foundation chain will have a series of little Vs. After you have made the foundation chain, count the stitches back from the hook. Insert the hook into the second V along the hook. Wrap the yarn around the hook and draw it back through this stitch. You will now have 2 loops on the hook. Wrap the YOH again and draw it through both loops on the hook. You have a made a single crochet! Continue into every stitch until you get to the end of the foundation row.

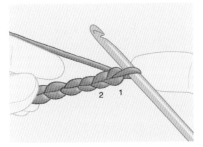

1. After you have made the foundation chain, count the stitches back from the hook. Insert the hook into the second V along the hook.

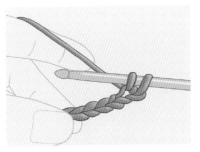

2. Wrap the yarn around the hook and draw it back through this stitch. You will now have 2 loops on the hook.

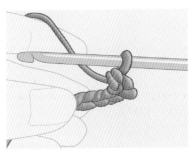

3. Wrap the YOH again and draw it through both loops on the hook. You have a made a double crochet! Continue into every stitch until the end of the foundation row.

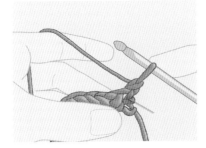

4. To work the next row, chain 1 and turn your work. Insert your hook into the first stitch under the top 2 loops and complete steps 2 and 3. Continue working double crochet stitches across the row. You do not work a stitch into the turning chain of the previous row.

Sewing Up

Mattress Stitch

A mattress stitch, sewn with a blunt tapestry needle, is the neatest and most discreet way to make a seam.

1. With right sides of both pieces of fabric toward you, secure yarn at the bottom of one piece. Pass needle to opposite section and insert needle through one stitch, which you can see on the needle in this picture. Pull yarn through gently. Take needle to the opposite section and insert needle through one stitch of this section.

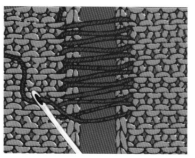

2. Continue in this way, from one side to the other as if lacing a corset, until you reach the last stitch. Secure tightly. If you have entered through the right section as shown opposite, the seam will be virtually indistinguishable from the rest of the fabric. Always be sure to use the same colour yarn as in the main body of work (the contrasting yarn in the picture is just to highlight the technique) so that when the seams are pulled and moved when worn, the joining yarn cannot be seen. Some yarns may be too weak to sew along a seam, so double them up, add a stronger yarn of the same colour.

Back Stitch

A back stitch is worked on the wrong side of the piece and gives a strong, neat finish.

1. With right sides together and wrong sides facing out, pin the seam together. Thread matching yarn on to a tapestry needle and join to one end of the seam by working a couple of stitches over the top of each other to secure the yarn end. Insert the needle down into the first layer and continue through the second layer then bring the needle back up through both layers, a few stitches along the seam. Pull yarn through. Insert the needle back into the same place as the first stitch then bring it back up through both layers a few stitches along from where it first came out.

2. Continue in this way along the seam, keeping your stitches even in size. When you reach the end of the seam, secure the yarn end by working a few stitches in the same place, then weave yarn end into work and trim.

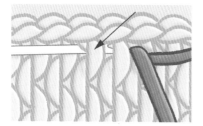

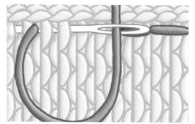

Weaving in Ends

After finishing your project you will have several yarn ends to weave into your work from casting on, casting off, changing colours or adding a new ball of yarn.

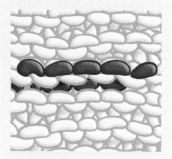

1. With wrong side of work facing, thread yarn end on to a tapestry needle and weave the yarn end in and out through the back of approximately 8 or 10 stitches along a row of stitches, then turn and work back in the opposite direction.

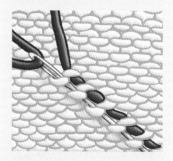

2. Alternatively, work diagonally up for a few rows, then back down to the original stitch, making sure nothing is visible from the right side. Where possible, weave ends into the seam stitches for approximately 8 to 10 stitches. Trim yarn end close to the work.

Embellishments

Pompoms

These are an easy way to bring a fun touch to hats and some of the hats featured in this book will use them for ears and other facial features.

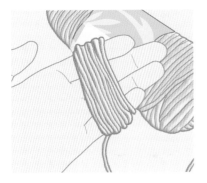  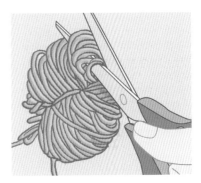

1. Wrap the yarn around a piece of cardboard or your fingers. Four fingers make a large pompom, three fingers make a medium pompom and two fingers make a small pompom. The more yarn you wrap, the fuller the pompom will be.

2. Carefully slide the pompom off the cardboard or your fingers. Take a long piece of the yarn and wrap it around the centre. Tie a knot tightly in the yarn and leave the ends of the knot long. You can use this to attach the pompom to your project later.

3. Cut through the folded loops on each side of the pompom with scissors. When you are finished cutting through the yarn, give the pompom a good shake, and then trim the ends to make a fluffy, rounded shape (see right).

Felt Appliqué Using a Whip Stitch

Some of the hats use felt appliqué for eyes, nostrils and other features. The neatest way to do this is to cut two pieces of felt for each part and whip stitch them together before stitching them to the hat. A whip stitch (shown below) is worked from the right side of the felt so the end result is visible. Using matching thread and small stitches reduces the visibility of the stitches.

Lay the two pieces of fabric together, one on top of the other with the wrong sides together and right sides facing out. Align the edges and pin, if necessary. Using a whip stitch, sew around the edges of the fabric until you reach the first stitch. Secure the seam with a knot on the wrong side of the work. Weave thread ends into the wrong side of thework and trim.

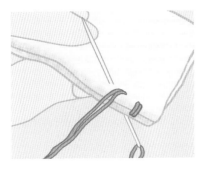

First two stitches.

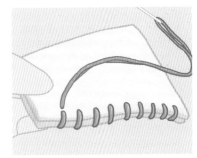

Nine stitches along.

Attaching a Fringe Using a Crochet Hook Technique

1. Cut the yarn into lengths of the same size. For a mane or Mohawk, 12 to 15cm (5 to 6in) is a good length. Take a length of yarn and fold in half. With the right sides of the hat facing out, push your crochet hook down into a stitch and up through the next stitch. Place the loop of the folded yarn over the hook and pull back through the stitches, so that the length of folded yarn is halfway through the stitches. The loop will be sticking out at one end, and the two ends will be sticking out at the other end.

2. Wrap the two ends of yarn around the crochet hook, and then pull the ends of yarn through the looped end.

3. Pull tight. One fringe is added. Repeat as necessary.

Braid

Some of the hats in this book are embellished with a braid of yarn attached to the earflaps or ribbed border. Essentially, a braid of yarn is a braided cord made from lengths of yarn. Cut 100cm (40in) strips of yarn as instructed in the pattern. This may be 12 or 16 strips of various colours. Using a crochet hook, pull the first 3 or 4 lengths of first colour halfway through a stitch where the braid begins. Next, pull 3 or 4 lengths of the second colour halfway through the next stitch along, and then pull the remaining 3 or 4 lengths of the first colour halfway through the next stitch along. You now have 6 or 8 pieces of yarn in each of the 3 sections. Secure the hat between your knees and braid the 3 sections of yarn together as follows.

1. * Keeping the 3 sections separate, bring the left section over the middle section. The left section is now the middle section.

2. Bring the right section over the middle section. The right section is now the middle section.

3 Repeat from * until your braid is the desired length. Make a knot at the end to secure the braids, and then trim the ends straight.

Twisted Cord

A twisted cord is quick and easy to make and does not involve any knitting. You can make them long or short, and they are useful for a lot of things including straps, ties and button fasteners. The cord is created by twisting yarn tightly, and the finished cord will be approximately one-quarter of the starting length of yarn.

1. To make a twisted cord take a piece of yarn 4 times the length of the finished cord. If you want a 15cm (6in) cord, cut a 60cm (24in) length of yarn. Fold the yarn in half and place the folded loop around a door handle or pin it securely to a cushion. Knot the two yarn ends together and place a pencil in this loop. Pull the yarn tight and start turning the pencil so that the yarn begins to twist.

2. Keep going until the twists are really tight and the cord starts to kink when the pencil is relaxed. Lift the yarn off the door handle or cushion carefully so that it does not unwind. Fold the cord in half, letting it twist around itself to make a thicker cord and knot the two ends together.

Index

Acknowledgements

Thanks to my family and friends for your encouragement, inspiration, and support – I'm forever in your debt. A huge thanks to Quintet Publishing for giving me this amazing opportunity and helping to turn my dreams into reality– with a special thanks to Margaret Swinson (project editor) for her patience and assistance.

I'd like to thank past and present editors of *Let's Get Crafting*, *Inside Crochet*, *Knit Today* and *Homemaker* magazines for publishing my work, for their continued support and for giving me the confidence to tackle my first book. Thanks also to the photographers and delightful models who have made my designs look absolutely amazing and super cute.

Thanks to my three children (Kate, Izzy and Ollie) for inspiring me, for putting up with my knitting adventures, and for acting as models for my knitwear. Ollie now has a long list of hats he'd like for himself.

Most of all I'd like to thank my husband Alex for his neverending patience and support, despite being busy with work himself. I'm pretty sure he'd be an expert knitter as he now knows the theory inside out. Thanks Alex for letting me pursue my dreams– you're a star.

Lynne

Models:
Alix Noirtin
Camille Noirtin
Laurie Searle
Romilly Searle
Sylvester Ellis
Audrey Harrison-Parsons
Conrad Bulle
Frieda Bulle
Akira Kozai
Eva Davies
Xavier Okaforr
Danielle Holbrook
Evie Martin
Harrison Cochrane-Hanley
Ivy Cochrane-Hanley
Marie-Francoise Wolff
Annabel Harding-Grant
Jovi Pincay
Tommy Maxwell
Loic Simpson
Quincy Williams
Zion Danso
Johan Van Der Looy

Clothing:
JoJo Maman Bebe
JoJo House
Cloisters Business Centre
8 Battersea Road
London
SW8 4BG